BAN-GUJARS

A Nomadic Tribe in Himachal Pradesh

BAN-GUJARS

A Nomadic Tribe in Himachal Pradesh

BAN-GUJARS

A Nomadic Tribe in Himachal Pradesh

V. Verma

B.R. Publishing Corporation
[A Division of BRPC (India) Ltd.]
Delhi-110035

Distributed by:

BRPC (India) Ltd.

4222/1, Ansari Road, Darya Ganj,
New Delhi-110002
Ph.: 3259196, 3259648
Fax: 3201571
E-Mail: *brpcltd@del2.vsnl.net.in*

ISBN 81-7646-112-1

Published by:

B.R. Publishing Corporation

[A Division of BRPC (India) Ltd.]
3779, Ist Floor, Kanhaiya Nagar,
Tri Nagar, Delhi-110035
Phone: 7152140
E-Mail: *brpcltd@del2.vsnl.net.in*

Rs. 500

Laser Typeset by:

Jain Media Graphics
Delhi-110035

Printed by:

PRAJA Offset
Delhi

PRINTED IN INDIA

Acknowledgements

I often say that no assignment would get very far without the support and assistance from others. Mian Govardhan Singh, my old friend, inspired and supported me through and through. Several other kind friends helped me with valuable suggestions and ideas. For their valuable contributions I especially thank Dr. O.P. Sharma of Dr. Y.S. Parmar University of Horticulture and Forestry, Solan and Dr. Bansi Ram Sharma. Shri Inder Pal, photographer, an artist of high repute, who would rather love to be known by the appellation of *pahari photographer,* has kindly permitted the use of photographs. The map is the handiwork of Vinod Rana and Ms. Veena Thakur. I am obliged to both of them. I am also beholden to Shri D.C. Jistu, the fruit of whose painstaking research, I have liberally used. Not included by name here are many others who have willingly and readily spent their time and energy to assist me. To all of them I am equally grateful.

I have consulted with profit numerous works of celebrated authors. I owe them respect and regards and gladly acknowledge it.

I record my warm gratitude to Shri Praveen Mittal of BRPC (India) Ltd. Without his personal interest this book would not have appeared so soon and so good in print.

I am appreciative of the strength and inspiration I have drawn from my dear wife, who has sustained me through thick and thin as also from my caring children and grandchildren.

Finally, I offer this book as my humble tribute to the simple, hardy and colourful people, who as some historians claim, are the proud descendants of Gurjaras, once a mighty and powerful autoethonous ruling race.

The Pines,   **V. Verma**
Panthaghati,
Kasumpti,
Shimla-171009.

Preface

In the north western part of India, the western Himalaya nurses the two most beautiful States of India. They are Jammu & Kashmir and Himachal Pradesh. The stunning grandeur of its mountains and the superb panorama makes this region a virtual paradise on earth. Nature has been abundantly generous but the anachronism amidst immense beauty lies in man, whose poverty knows no bounds nor does his pain and misery. The allusion is to the Gujars, the nomads in the region. Some, especially the Hindu Gujars, have since long settled down and live in symbiosis with the local peasantry. Some of them still combine agriculture, their main occupation, with their past vocation of herding buffaloes in the wastes adjoining their settlements. The Muhammadan Gujars or the *ban* or forest Gujars (of Jammu stock), however, possess neither house nor cultivate land. They have virtually no notion of a definite 'home land' within or outside of Himachal Pradesh. It is from their wandering buffalo herds that they obtain their livelihood, primarily selling milk, butter and clarified butter (ghi). Their extensive migratory movements take them to fairly remote areas of the State. Interestingly even in these almost inaccessible places, the traders manage to reach in order to purchase ghi and cheat them.

Unlike the Gaddis, another pastoral community of Chamba, the Gujars entered the region at a relatively late period. Their somewhat more recent appearance in the State is indicated by their failure to obtain permanent grazing rights in the forests and pastures of the State. In Chamba, Kangra and some other lower areas though they seem to have established some loose kind of *warisi*. In Mandi State Gazetteer too one comes across a reference to Muhammadan Gujars spending 'the entire year moving seasonally from one pasture to pasture'. Along with grazing came numerous forest and grazing laws. A network of rights, obligations and dues was created by the enactment of these laws. Apart from raising revenue for the State coffer, another important object sought to be obtained was to maintain a balance between the varying interests often clashing, of pastoralists, the domestic graziers and the forests and pastures.

By the beginning of the twentieth century the mounting pressure on grazing land came to be noticed. Quite possibly the uncontrolled increase in the number of livestock owned both by the land-holding gentry and the pastoralists was responsible for it. The 'undoubted deterioration of the Kangra forests', it was perceived, was due to 'over-grazing'. On his tour of Kangra district in 1911, J. Douie, the Financial Commissioner, suggested reduction in the number of cattle as the only remedy. Implementation of new forest policies and the classification of extensive areas as reserved forests has ever since sought to restrict the grazing area and the livestock though without much success. With no political clout at their disposal, the *ban* Gujars and their buffalo herds have become the scapegoat.

This book attempts to portray their tribal world covering their origin and history, socio-cultural, economic and religious life and also makes certain suggestions in respect of the manner of their gradual integration into the mainstream.

I hope that this small volume will not fail to interest a variety of people – social workers, planners, administrators, anthropologists – and all those interested in the tribal segment of India mosaic.

The Pines,   **V. Verma**
Panthaghati,
Kasumpti,
Shimla-171009.

Contents

Contents

List of Photographs

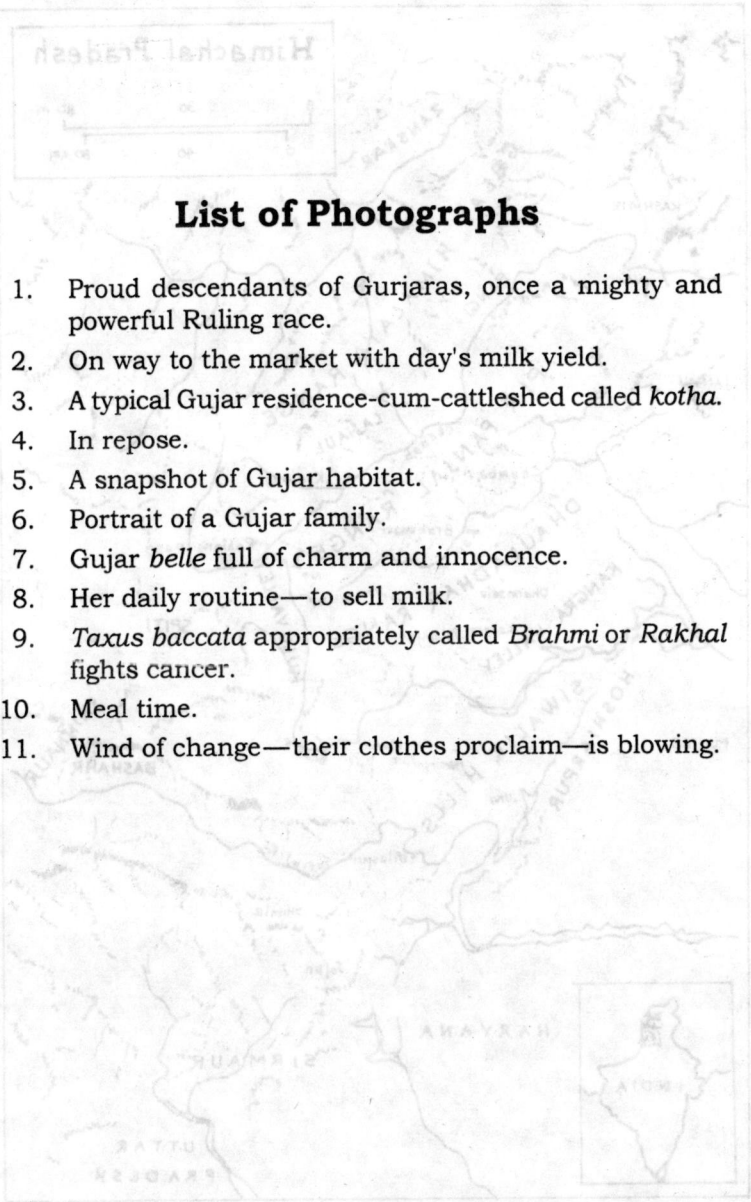

Himachal Pradesh

KASHMIR

ZANSKAR

JAMMU

GREAT HIMALAYA RANGE

PANGI

PIR PANJAL RANGE

Chenab

LAHAUL

Chamba

Kyelong

Brahmaur

Rohtang pass

DHAULADHAR RANGE

Dharmsala

KULU VALLEY

KANGRA VALLEY

Kangra Palampur

SPITI

PUNJAB

SIWALIK HILLS

Mandi

KINNAUR

Hamirpur

Beas R.

HOSHIARPUR

Una

BASHAHR

Bilaspur

Sutlej R.

Shimla

Solan

INDIA

HARYANA

SIRMAUR

UTTAR PRADESH

Evolution of Transhumant Grazing

1

Himachal Pradesh—Land and the People

Historical Perspective

Tucked in the lap of western Himalaya, no other region of Indian Union, with the sole exception of Jammu and Kashmir, extends as far north as does the State of Himachal Pradesh. Extending for nearly three latitude degrees and longitude between 30°.22' N and 33°.10' north of the equator and 75°.46' to 79° east of Greenwich, the prime meridian, Himachal Pradesh extends from the Siwalik hills in the south to the great Himalayan ranges including a slice of Trans-Himalaya, in the north. Hedged in between the Ravi river in the west and the Yamuna in the east, it spreads out for a length of 355 kms from the north-western extremity of Chamba to the south-eastern tip of Kinnaur. Breadth-wise it extends for 270 kms from Kangra in near south-west to Kinnaur in the near north-east occupying a total area of 55,673 sq. kms.

Himachal Pradesh is an ancient land, so old that its early history is shrouded in mystery. Recent archaeological surveys conducted by Prof. B.B. Lal[1] and R.V. Joshi[2] trace it to the later stage of Paleolithic period. 'There is no doubt that human habitation had been established (in this region) long before the Aryan infiltration.'[3] The Indus Valley civilization (3000-1,750 B.C.) covered the whole of Punjab. Its extension into the Himalayan foothills resulted in the Munda speaking Kalorian people being pushed into the vastness of the Himalayas including into the region presently forming Himachal Pradesh. The Vedas recognise these people as *dasas, dasyus, nishad, kols or mundas.* They were perhaps the earliest immigrants to settle in Himachal hills. Possibly the *kolis, halis, dums* and *chanals* of the Western Himalaya and *chamang* and *damang* of Kinnaur are the descendants of that aborigine race. *Bhotas* and *Kiratas,* these days found mostly in and around Kinnaur, Lahul and Spiti,[4] historically are believed to have immigrated thereafter into the sub-Himalayan region. *Khasas,* a war-like tribe, is known to have preceded the Vedic Aryans, who in course of time converted the entire territory from Kinnaur to Nagaland into the *khasa* land. Mahabharta (1,000 B.C.) and Panini (500 B.C.) speak of *Janapadas* like the Audumbaras, the Trigarta, the Kulatas, the Kunindas and the Yaudheyas ruled by these people. The kingdom of Trigarta, the land of three rivers, (the Sutlej, the Ravi and the Beas) comprised all the country between the Sutlej and the Ravi including the *Jalandhar doab* in the plains: Kangra then called Bhimkot was its hill capital. Katoch dynasty founded by Susarma Chandra traces its lineage to the Mahabharta age. 'While our ancestors were unreclaimed savages and while the Empire of Rome was yet in its infancy, there was a Katoch monarchy with an organized government at Kangra' observe Col. Jenkin and Harcourt to show its great antiquity. Lepel Griffin refers to the Rajput dynasties of the hills, of whom the Katoch was the oldest, as having 'geneologies more ancient and unbroken than can be shown by any other royal families in the world.'[5] Hiuen Tsang's travel accounts speak very highly of the kingdom of Jalandhar. Of its riches and greatness Ferishta says 'priests and princes used vessels of silver and gold and were dressed in embroidered silk. History and philosophy were studied and commentaries written on books older than the Assyrian empire.'[6]

The eventual collapse of the Vardhana empire saw the emergence of a number of petty chiefs, the Ranas and Thakurs, who established territories of diminutive sizes, all being liable to constant change as one ruler gained ascendancy over another. The feudal lords in turn were subdued by the Rajput families who were attempting to reconsolidate their strength in the hills in the eleventh century, having fled from the Indo-Gangetic plains under attack by the Turks. The complex topographical features of Himachal, however, rendered it impossible for any one ruler to establish control over the whole region. Only small states could exist, and these enjoyed varying degrees of independence. A few important were Jaswan, Guler (off-shoot of Kangra), Siba (off-shoot of Guler) and Datarpur (off-shoot of Suket), Bilaspur (Kahloor), Nalagarh (Hindur), Kutlehar and Baghal. Most of the territory between Sutlej and Yamuna was under the chiefs of Bushahr and Sirmaur; the rest parcelled out amongst a number of petty chieftains, recognised under the appellation of *bara thakurais* and *athara thakurais*. Keonthal, Bhagat, Kunihar, Kuthar, Bhajji, Dhami, Mahlog, Koti, Mangal, Bija, Bharoli and Baghal were tributaries of Kahloor or Sirmaur, who-so-ever happened to command their allegiance according to the degree of power it wielded at any given point of time. The *athara thakurais* of which Jubbal, Balsan, Theog, Kumarsain, Darkoti, Tharoch, Sangri, were prominent, were located in the valleys of Sutlej, Giri and Pabbar rivers.

This mountainous area did not witness any material political change during the Turkish invasions and the reigns of Tughlaq and Lodis save for odd raids from the Sultans, who were primarily engaged in the subjugation of the plains. These forays were conducted chiefly to pillage the legendary wealth stored in the temples and forts of the Katoch kingdom of Kangra, then the most prosperous among the hill dominions. This loot-and-retire policy underwent a radical change with the coming in power of Mughals, whose famous kings Akbar and Jahangir made serious attempts to expand their empire over this hilly country.

The Chamba State was one of the oldest native principalities in northern India. Sheltered by snow-clad mountain barriers, it had the rare fortune of escaping successive waves of foreign invaders. Like the Kangra chiefs, the Chamba rulers too paid tribute to the Mughals and so did the Sirmaur Rajas. Protected by hills and mountains and for lack of any strategic significance, the imperial authority sat lightly on these hill States, and the Mughal supremacy was only shadowy. The petty chieftains holding numerous territorial slices between Sutlej and Yamuna remained immune from Muhammadan overlordship of the Delhi empire, mainly because of the inaccessibility of these mountain enclaves.

On the death of Aurangzeb, the political situation deteriorated chiefly because of the rising power of the Marathas, the Afghans and the Jats. Nadir Shah and Ahmad Shah dwelt death blows to the tottering Delhi empire. Slackening of Mughal authority afforded the Katoch ruler, Ghamand Chand, a god-sent opportunity to rebel and occupy his ancestral Kangra kingdom. By A.D. 1,773 Maharaja Sansar Chand, his grand-son, whose claim as a great patron of fine arts and crafts stands unrivalled in the history of Himachal Pradesh, became the supreme ruler in the region. During his reign the hill kingdom witnessed its golden period. Having subjugated all the surrounding hill states, Sansar Chand, a man of considerable ambition cast a covetous eye on the fertile Jalandhar *doab*. Here, however, he had to contend against Maharaja Ranjit Singh, the formidable chief of mighty Sikh power and a terror of Punjab. Two years later he was badly mauled by the Gurkhas who laid waste his entire country. Such devastating was the loot and plunder that 'not a blade of cultivation was to be seen and grass grew up in the towns and tigresses whelped in the streets of Nadaun.'[7] In the clash between the Sikhs and the Gurkhas, the later had to retreat leaving Ranjit Singh in control of the whole of Kangra. In 1,846 A.D. on its rout at their hands, the Sikh Durbar ceded to the British in perpetuity the whole of the *doab* between Sutlej and the Beas. Sequel to the treaty, the hill states of Kangra, Guler, Jaswan, Datarpur, Nurpur, Suket, Mandi, Kullu and Lahul and Spiti passed under the British domination. The Rajas of Bilaspur and Nalagarh had already pledged their allegiance to the British. The Chamba state, whose territory formed part of the hill country transferred to Maharaja Gulab Singh of Jammu, was later restored to British suzerainty in exchange for Bhadrwah.

Thrown out of Kangra, Gurkhas directed their attention towards Shimla hills and after defeating the local chiefs soon became master of the entire country lying between Yamuna and Sutlej. In 1,814 war broke out between Nepal and the

British. In the military compaign in this region, Amar Singh Thapa, the Gurkha general was defeated and had to surrender to the British the entire hill country from Kali to Sutlej. The local chiefs, who had assisted the British were by and large restored to their possessions in pursuance of the British proclamation 'inviting co-operation of the chiefs and the people' and assuring withdrawal 'from that part of the country after the matter had been restored to the condition before the Gurkha invasion.'[8]

Himachal Pradesh at present comprises the territories of all the Punjab Hill States and the districts of Kangra, Kullu, Shimla and Lahul and Spiti and certain parts of Hoshiarpur, Gurdaspur and Ambala districts, awarded to it under the Punjab Re-organisation Act 1966, in addition to the territories exchanged *vide* The Provinces and States (Absorption of Enclaves) Order, 1950.[9]

Physical Geography

Himachal Pradesh lies enmeshed in the folds of the great Himalaya, which in the words of poet Kalidasa (in *Kumarsambhava)* is the king of all the mountains in the world and whose divine soul, Swami Vivekananda, has described as laying down the standard to judge by all other human civilizations, from the pre-historical to the modern.

All the way from the Pamir plateau and the Indus valley near Nanga Parbat in the west to the great pillar of Namcha Barwa near the Brahmputra bend in the east, the Himalaya, stretches for about 3,000 kilometres. It is the greatest physical feature on earth: though the highest on the planet, it is geologically the youngest. The Himalayan system is believed to have risen from the bed of a pre-historic ocean called Tethys some fifty million years ago, due to successive episodes of tectonic activity, each distinct phase forming a mountain chain different from the other. The mighty Himalaya, oriented in south-westerly direction forms a gigantic crescentic crown over the Indian sub-continent lying in its lap on the north. This curvature is abruptly sharp towards the western segment, where the Himalaya is at its widest and hence likened to a scimitar. It is this particular portion of the system which has come to be called the

Western Himalaya. This vast expanse of mountainous and sub-mountainous territory is bounded by the Indus in the extreme west and the Tons-Jamuna gorges in the east. The whole western Himalayan tract is approximately situated between 75° and 80° due east and 30° and 36° due north.

The northern Himalayan belt starting from Arunachal Pradesh in the east to Lahul and Spiti (in Himachal Pradesh) and Ladakh (Jammu and Kashmir) in the west is geographically divided into three distinct regions-the Eastern, the Central and the Western. Himachal Pradesh is a generous section of the western region and its boundaries, generally speaking, coincide with the Jalandhar *khanda* of Puranic concept. Five successive mountain ranges, wrinkles in an ageing land, curve across the State. From south to north, these are the Siwaliks, the Dhauladhar, the Pir Panjal, the Great Himalaya and the Zaskar. Below the Siwaliks stretch the dusty plains of Punjab and at an elevated plane beyond the Zaskar mountains lies the arid plateau of Tibet.

Those mountain ranges which attain an altitude of 5,000 to 6,500 metres above sea level are called the Great Himalaya. In Himachal Pradesh lies its eastern extension. The Pir Panjal range joins it near Deo Tiba. Between these two is tucked the valley of Lahul : the range is cut across by the gorge of the Sutlej river and divides the Spiti and Beas drainage systems. The passes of Parang (5,548 m), Kangra (5,248 m), Pin Parbati (4,802 m), Baralacha (4,512 m) and Kunzum (5,248 m) are prominent and Lahul, inaccessible in winter, is reached through Rohtang pass (4,361 m) on the Pir Panjal.

To the east lies Zaskar range also called Inner Himalaya. It separates the basin of Tibet from Himachal Pradesh and connects it with the Sutlej basin through the passes of Sholarung and Gumrang. Sutlej cuts this range through a gorge at Shipki. The Sutlej basin is rugged and snowy; the adjoining Spiti is the museum of geological formations with continuous record of sedimentary rocks found no elsewhere else in the Himalaya. The Great Himalayan range crosses the Sutlej valley near Chini and Kalpa; Kinner Kailash is the highest peak (6,473 m). In the east a highrise dissected plateau is centered at Pooh where one comes across myriad remnants of past glaciation.

The Lesser Himalaya with an average elevation of 4,000 to 5,000 metres sits between the Greater Himalaya and Siwalik ranges. Series of its parallel ranges are interspersed by longitudinal valleys, the sole exception being Kullu valley; running at right angles it is transverse to the main lay-out. Kangra valley is longitudinal trough or depression at the foot of the Dhauladhar (Dhavala[10] giri). Dhauladhar soars up majestically in an abrupt sweep to 4,930 metres, forming a formidable obstacle in the path of low-flying south-westerly rain-laden monsoon clouds, which perforce lighten their vaporous burden before rising high to proceed northwards. Southern slopes of Dhauladhar are thus one of the wettest places in the subcontinent. This range roughly marks the boundary between the two adjoining districts of Kangra and Chamba and forms a most idyllic backdrop. 'Few spots in the Himalayas for beauty or grandeur can compare with the Kangra valley and these over-shadowing hills'. Enchanted Mr. Barnes, wrote of it[11]:

> No scenery, in my opinion, presents such sublime and delightful contrasts. Below lies the plain, a picture of rural loveliness and repose; the surface is covered with the richest cultivation irrigated by streams which descend from perennial snows, and interspersed with homesteads buried in the midst of groves and fruit trees. Turning from this scene of peaceful beauty, the stern and majestic hills confront us; their sides are furrowed with precipitous water-courses; forests of oak clothe their flanks, and higher up give place to gloomy and funereal pines; above all are wastes of snow, or pyramidal masses of granite too perpendicular for the snow to rest on.

The northern slope of the Dhauladhar range is set against the southern slope of Pir Panjal: the average elevation of the later range is 4,600 metres above sea level. Beas has cut awe-inspiring gorges in Dhauladhar at Larji and Aut, and about 300 metres deep but only 10 metres wide at Kothi at the foot of Pir Panjal in an I-shaped gorge.

The outermost sandstone frontal ranges of the western Himalaya are the Siwaliks, called *Mainak Parbat* by the ancient geographers. The range roughly marks a natural border between the plains of the Punjab and the hills of Himachal Pradesh. Steeper towards the plains and ascending gently northwards they form wide and undulating basins, the *duns*, of unsurpassable grandeur and charm with verdant vales, gurgling streams and tranquil lakes set in their luxuriant best.

Relief

Himachal Pradesh is veiled from the Punjab plains by Siwalik hills. It is a hilly and mountainous tract with altitudes ranging from about 450 m to 6,500 m above sea level. The region presents an intricate mosaic of mountain ranges, hills and valleys. The white snow-clad peaks are its most prominent landmark. The Dhauladhar range looks in supreme majesty over the Kangra valley while the Pir Panjal, the Great Himalayan and the Zaskar ranges stand guard over Chamba, Lahul and Spiti, Kullu and Kinnaur. The majestic array of sky-kissing peaks is visible from far and wide. The mountain slopes are covered with forests and meadows. The peaceful valleys below are interspersed with numerous streams, fields and quaint homesteads. The rolling downs are strewn with boulders. Seen from a vantage point the lower hills appear like ripples of the sea suddenly arrested and frozen into stones. 'Nowhere in the world the small natural regions are more sharply separated than in the Himalaya' observes Kangra District Gazetteer.

There are indications of extensive glaciation during the Ice Age and the present glaciers are merely 'shrunken remnants'. Enormous heaps of terminal moraines, now grass and tree covered, ice-transported blocks with smoothened and striated surfaces, hanging and U-shaped valleys and glacial lakes are notable features of the past glaciation. In Pir Panjal above 2,000 m the mountains have a glaciated aspect while the valleys are filled with moraines and fluvio-

glacial drift. 'On the southern slopes of Dhauladhar range
an old moraine is found at such an extraordinary low altitude
as 3,660', while in some parts of Kangra, glaciers were at
the time believed, though not on good evidence, to have
descended to 3,000 ft. level.'[12] There are numerous river
terraces observed near Kangra, Mandi and Kullu.

Drainage

In the furrows between these ranges flow perennial rivers
which drain the snow-capped slopes into the Indus system.
This roughly rectangular mountain region contains the
basins of four great rivers—the Ravi (*Vedic*-Parushni, *Skt.*
Iravati), the Beas (*Vedic*-Aritkiya, *Skt.* Vipasa), the Chenab
(*Vedic*-Asikni), and the Sutlej (*Vedic*-Satudri, *Skt.* Shatadru).
Besides, Yamuna, the largest tributary of the Ganga system,
also drains a part of the region.

Ravi drains the watershed of the Bara Banghal massive.
Threading its way through the trough between the Pir Panjal
and Dhauladhar, more or less, in westerly direction, Ravi
pierces the later range to turn south towards Punjab. It
flows past the Chamba town and divides the district into
two unequal halves.

The eastern ramparts of the Bara Banghal feed the Beas,
which gathers its headwaters from this transverse rib as
well as from the southern slopes of Pir Panjal near Rohtang
pass. The Bara Banghal forces the river to flow in a southerly
direction through Kullu till it pushes its way through
Dhauladhar barrier at Larji, carrying along, the waters of
its main tributaries, the Parbati, the Hurla, the Sainj and
the Tirthen. Meandering through the Siwaliks it is joined in
the foothills by the Uhl, the Suketi, the Luni, the Awa, the
Banganga, the Gaj and the Chakki.

Lahul, the major defile between the Pir Panjal and the
Great Himalayan range forms the basin of the Chenab. The
largest river of the State (in volume of water), it is a joint
stream of the Chandra and Bhaga, originating from the
opposite sides of Bara Lacha at an elevation of 4,900 m. It
flows through the famous Pangi tract of Chamba in a north-
westerly direction for 122 km before forcing its passage

through the Pir Panjal in Kishtwar. The 1,200 kms long Chenab has a catchment area of 7,500 kms within the State.

The Sutlej, the largest tributary of the Indus, is unique in that it rises in the distant highlands of Tibet beyond Himalaya. It enters Himachal Pradesh through a notch in the Zaskar range at Shipki and carves awesome gorges first through the Dhauladhar, 'forming perhaps the most striking physical feature of the region.[13] In the gap between the Zaskar and the Great Himalaya, the Sutlej is joined from the north-west by Spiti, one of its major tributaries, and Baspa, which joins it just unstream of the gorge. After crossing the Great Himalayan range, Sutlej flows, more or less, in a south-west direction before emerging in the plains of Punjab.

The Yamuna rises in Yamunotri from a hot-water spring in Uttar Kashi (Uttar Pradesh), just below the *Bandarpunchh* group of snowy peaks. The river flows in a south-west direction upto Banog and then turns west. At Kalsi it is met by the Tons, its principal tributary. Giri and Bata join it upstream and down-stream of Paonta Sahib. It moves out of Himachal Pradesh near Tajewala headworks. Its catchment area in Himachal Pradesh totals 2,320 kms.

Because of the alignment of the Lesser ranges being oblique to the Great Himalaya, the basins of the rivers in Himachal Pradesh are asymmetrical and also oblique to the Great Himalayan alignment.

Climate

Situated in the north-west of the sub-continent, over 1,600 km removed from the Bay of Bengal and lying between the Greater Himalaya in the north and the Punjab plains in the south, Himachal Pradesh experiences extremely varied climatic conditions principally due to variation in elevation and the aspect. In general the climate of the State is distinguished from the adjoining Punjab plains by colder and prolonged winters, comparatively heavier precipitation and shorter and less oppressive summers. Its two main climatic characteristics are the seasonal rhythm of weather and the vertical zoning. The southern sandy foothill tracts and the plain areas experience hot and sub-humid tropical climate. With the increase in altitude the climate changes from temperate to cold alpine and somewhat arctic condition: altitude the most significant factor controlling the climate. Based on the principle of lapse rate the low valley bottoms and the areas lying below 600 m above sea level have hot and moist tropical climate. The areas above 600 m but below 2,000 m experience cool temperate climate. Higher up, it is cold temperate upto an elevation of 3,000 m. Further up the temperature falls down rapidly till one reaches the snow line. Above the snow line the climate changes from arctic to polar type according as the altitude is. Because of interplay of aspect the south-facing slopes are sunny and rainier and those towards north are comparatively dry, fall as they generally do in rain shadow. As these are warmed by slanting sun rays, the northern slopes are relatively cold as well.

Difference in aspect and altitude gives rise to microclimates. In general, however, the climatic zones range from sub-tropical (450-900 m) to warm temperate (900-1,800 m), cool temperate (1,800-2,400 m), cold high mountain (2,400-4,000 m) and snowy and frigid (above 4,000 m). Cut off by the high mountain ranges, Lahul, Spiti and Kinnaur has semi-arid highland type of climate.

The distribution of rainfall varies from less than 780.1 mm (1993) in greater part of Lahul and Spiti to over 3,400 mm at Dharamsala. Generally it increases from the plains to the hills according to relief and aspect. Beyond Kullu the rainfall decreases due to rain-shadow effect. In all places below 900 m heat is excessive during summer, the highest monthly maximum temperature experienced in June. It snows during winter down to an elevation of about 1,500 m but the snow does not lie for long below 2,500 m. At elevations of above 3,000 m the average snowfall is about 3 m and lasts for 4 months, from December to March. Above 4,500 m there is almost perpetual snow. The lowest monthly minimum temperature is experienced during January. The relative humidity is generally higher during the pre-monsoon and monsoon period. After September it declines sharply. During winter the values are lower and continue to remain so till April. Mandi is an exception. Here the humidity is generally high; situated as it is, on the river Beas in a more or less hill-enclosed basin.

Natural Vegetation

There is striking diversity in natural vegetation caused primarily by varying altitudes, natural conditions like temperature, rainfall and pattern of climate ranging from sub-tropical to cold temperate. Changes are also attributed to site and soil factors, angle and aspect of slopes as well as by the history of biotic interference. On the whole, the Outer Himalaya type of vegetation carries the influence of monsoon; towards the Inner Himalaya of winter precipitation; and in the far north along the fringe of Tibet of dry and arid climate.

Owing to a wide range of altitude and climatic conditions, Himachal Pradesh has a rich west Himalayan flora; in diversity varying from Himalayan meadows and high level birch and rhododendron to tropical scrub and bamboo forests of the low hills. The Himachal forests cover an area of 3,540,705 hec. *i.e.*, 66.57 per cent of the total geographical area. Variously classified they occupy:

1.	Reserved forests	Hec.	189613
2.	Protected forests	Hec.	3147244
3.	Unclassed forests	Hec.	68038
4.	Other forests	Hec.	40421
5.	Forests not under the control of Forest Department	Hec.	95389
	Total	Hec.	3540705

Forests, however, are not uniformly distributed throughout the region and are mostly confined to higher hills and interior valleys. In the lower and more accessible areas these have been cleared mostly for cultivation and settlement.

Statistics for the year 1996 released by the Himachal Pradesh Forest Department puts the forest cover by different types at 12,501 sq. kms., *viz.*,

Tropical diciduous forests	2272 sq. km.
Tropical thorn forests	45 sq. km.
Sub-Tropical Pine forests	4088 sq. km.
Sub-Tropical Dry Ever-green forests	500 sq. km.
Himalayan Moist Temperate forests	4313 sq. km.
Sub-Alpine and Alpine forests	1283 sq. km.

The natural vegetation has a climatic latitudinal zonation. In area it is distributed as below:

Below 1000 metres	sq. km.	10554
Between 1000-1500 metres	sq. km.	5793
Between 1500-2500 metres	sq. km.	7779
Between 2500-3000 metres	sq. km.	4995
Between 3000-4000 metres	sq. km.	7551
Above 4000 metres	sq. km.	19001
	sq. km.	55673

Dr. S.L. Kayastha has classified the forests of the region into nine forest types. These are:

(i) **Dry Alpine** forests are mainly found in Kinnaur, Lahul-Spiti and Pangi. They are very open xerophytics. Juniper, artemesia, lonicera, cotoneaster, etc., are the main species found in this belt. Extensive alpine pastures are the characteristic feature which found interspersing the forests support large flocks of sheep and goats during summer months. At some places aromatic shrubs too are found.

(ii) **Moist Alpine Scrub** forests are met with above the tree line but below the snow-line. Generally grass is found on the southern aspect and scrubs on the northern. Many plants grow in the rocky fissures and chasms alongwith sweet edible berries. The belt is fairly rich in herbaceous flora and other medicinal herbs and plants like *guggal, karu* and *aconite.* The alpine grasses provide nutritive grazing grounds. Main species found are salix, lonicera, viburnum, etc.

(iii) **Sub-Alpine** forests occur below the moist alpine scrub forests but above the altitude of 3,500 m. *Kharsu* and *betula utlis* are the typical trees of this zone. Dwarf birches and conifers are also found scattered in these forests. High level blue pine occurs in parts of Kinnaur, Pangi and Lahul. These are generally well stocked between 2,800-3,800 m. Between 2,500-4,000 m occur the Himalayan Temperate Parklands which are characterised by grasslands having scattered misshapen and often moribund trees of *kharsu* oak, maple, etc. These pastures stay buried under the snow all through the winter months. When the snow melts by the end of March, the tops of the hills, which are moderately flat and open, become covered with verdure affording splendid grazing for animals. The grass growing there is considered to be extremely nourishing and invigorating so much so that a few days' grazing refreshes and fattens the jaded and famished animals. Such ideal conditions for pasturage at such heights are possible on account of high humidity due to altitude and the gentle slope and impermeability of the rocks. The growth of seemingly inexhaustable quantity of succulent vegetation highly favours the nomads and their animals.

(iv) **Himalayan Moist Temperate and Mixed** forests occupy as a whole large area between 1,500-3,500 m. *Cedrus deodara* is the most valuable specie of these forests. Its principal concentrations are found in Chopal, Shimla, Kotgarh, Kinnaur, Suket, Nachan, Kullu, Seraj, Chamba and Churah divisions. In the Baspa valley *cedrus lebani* is found with magnificent girth upto 11 m. Chinar is also observed in association with *deodar* particularly in the Kullu and Parbati valleys. The upper oak, silver fir forests are met with between 3,000 and 3,500 m. Alder extends upto 2,250 m colonizing unstable hill sides and moist ravines. *Kail* occurs between 1,500-2,500 m mainly in Chopal, Pabar, Shimla, Kotgarh, Suket, Nachan, Mandi, Seraj, Kullu, Chamba and Kinnaur divisions. Pure spruce, pure silver-fir spruce and spruce *deodar* concentrations are found in areas of mixed coniferous forests.

(v) **Wet Temperate** forests are chiefly confined to wet slopes of Dalhousie, Dharamsala, Kangra and Jogindernagar areas. These include various temperate species like *chil* and *kail.* Deodar is also found in association with these two trees at many places. Bamboo groves are come across on the lower wet slopes.

(vi) **Sub-Tropical Pine** forests: Pure stands of sub-tropical pines (*Pinus Roxburgchi*) occur extensively in areas with elevation between 1,000 to 2,200 m. Lower or Siwalik *chil*-pine and Himalayan *chil*-pine occur extensively in Suket, Chamba, Nachan, Mandi, Bilaspsur, Kotgarh, Shimla, Chopal, Kangra, Nurpur, Dehra, Hamirpur and Una divisions. It dominates to the exclusion of any other associate. Very few shrubs occur as undergrowth. Resin is extensively tapped in these forests. Now oak plantations are coming up at certain areas.

(vii) **Sub-Tropical Broad Leaved** Hill forests stretch east to west from Mandi along the Beas (below 1,200 m). Great damage has been done to these forests by over-grazing and excessive lopping. Tall grasses, bamboos and shrubs have appeared where forests have been cleared by man.

(viii) **Northern Tropical Dry Deciduous** forests occur upto 1,250 m in the lower hills extending in the interior valleys along the rivers. *Shorea robusta* or *sal* is the main specie occurring in these forests, in particular, in Nahan and Bharwain. Other tropical deciduous species found are *simal* (*Bombax malabaricm*). Much of these forests have been cleared for cultivation and settlement. Grasses and bamboos grow in these clearings.

(ix) **Tropical Thorny** forests occupy small areas of Nalagarh, Pachhad and Una divisions. The dry vegetation consists of *acacia* trees (*babul, khair, phalahi*). These forests occur in well defined habitats like dry river courses, rock screes and bad lands created by excessive erosion on foot-hills.

Forests undoubtedly are of great importance from the point of economy as also ecology. Unfortunately damage to natural vegetation has been large and widespread. Deforestation has led to micro-climatic changes—loss of wild life, land-slips, erosion, lowering of sub-soil water level and irregular river regimes, all leading to serious environmental degradation. In these mountains serious deforestation and man-made soil erosion have occurred almost entirely since the mid-nineteenth century. Before then human settlement in the region was sparse and concentrated in the river valleys below 2,500 m. Even today the population of Himachal Pradesh is overwhelmingly rural, over ninety per cent living outside its few scattered towns. Before the economic expansion, which accompanied the colonial era, the forests were exploited lightly, and only close to villages or to major rivers where timber could easily be floated downstream. Grazing land was far more extensive than the needs of its livestock population. The 1850s and 1860s were the periods when commercial timber cutting started putting intense pressure on non-agricultural land. Uncontrolled cutting by contractors, plus expanding grazing in the forests newly cut, together, has led to a crisis of forest and pasture management. The result is what Parmar has uncompromisingly asserted:

> . . . these graziers with their large flocks, which
> are ever on the increase, have always been
> conspicuous enemies of the forests particularly in
> hill tracts. In a forest tract, in which their flocks
> graze in a concentrated manner or through which
> they pass, undergrowth vanishes, regeneration is
> no more, seedlings are eaten away, shrubs and
> bushes are munched and even the saplings cannot
> escape uninjured . . .
>
> (Parmar, 1959: 14)

The alarm bell has been ringing persistently ever since Himachal Pradesh has come into existence. The condition of permanent pastures, which was far from good in the early fifties, has considerably deteriorated since. They continue to be badly affected by excessive incidence of grazing by ever-mounting number of live-stock. Heavy soil erosion, which has set in as a consequence, is aggravating the grim situation. As an example, the high and low alpine pastures of Lahul, where more than eighty per cent of grazing runs were once considered overly rich in alpine nutritious grasses to-day lie badly mauled. According to a rough estimate as much as half of these pastures have badly-turned soil; intervening blanks under scrub and have unpalatable grasses for most of the time.

Soils

Himachal Pradesh is a land of young mountain soils, varying greatly even in areas of uniform climate and land forms: no sooner there is any change in the grade of slopes or in the site factor, the profile and characteristics of the soils change. Soils are the basic resource of the agricultural and pastoral economy of Himachal Pradesh. And 'soils must be used in such a way that production can be maintained at the desired level without soil deterioration or erosion while using crops which are particularly adapted to the existing soil conditions. This can be achieved through soil classification.'[14] Traditionally the yield and the productivity of crops have been adopted as ultimate criteria of soil classification. From this view point, top grade valley soils are deep, level and most productive; second grade soils are marked on gentle slopes; third grade soils can be used regularly by adopting a good crop rotation pattern and fourth grade soils occupy a marginal situation and suffer from many handicaps. The next four classes being situate on too steep slopes are not suitable for crop cultivation and are for grazing and forestry. And finally the soil on high mountains is suitable for nothing but wild life who subsist on its green cover. Focusing more on fertility status the Himachal Pradesh Agriculture department has classified the soils of the region into five major types.

(i)   *Low Hill Soil Zone*

It extends upto an elevation of 900 m and covers the areas of Kangra valley, Una, Hamirpur, Bilaspur, Nalagarh and the southern parts of Nahan and Paonta. Here the soils are shallow and embedded with stones. The *chos*, at some places, have deposited vast expanse of coarse sand. Alluvial soil is found only at certain favoured spots in valley bottoms along the river courses. This alluvium is quite suitable for rice, wheat and vegetable growing.

*(ii) **Mid-Hill Soil Zone***

This zone extends between 900 to 1,500 m and covers the tracts of eastern Chopal, eastern Renuka, north-western Nahan, Pachhad, Solan, Kandaghat, Arki and a thin belt along the lower heights of Dhauladhar. The soils of greyish-brown colour, loam to clay-loam in texture, are well drained. These soils are suitable for the cultivation of maize, wheat and tobacco. Fodder crops can also be raised successfully on these soils, which are rich in iron, potash, carbon and nitrogen but lack lime and phosphorous.

*(iii) **High Hill Soil Zone***

These soils extending between 1,500-2,100 m have developed on steep slopes with good drainage. Soil texture ranges from silty-loam to clay-loam with dark brown colour. These soils are found in the regions of Renuka, Chopal, Shimla, Sundernagar, Mandi and in a thin belt along the higher reaches of Dhauladhar. These soils are favourable for inferior grains, grasses and fodder crops. Where deeper, successful cultivation of potatoes, beans, maize and vegetables is carried on.

*(iv) **Mountain Soil Zone***

These soils are shallower in depth than the high hill soils: soil texture is silty-loam to loam of dark to light brown colour. These soils are found between 2,100-3,000 m in Jubbal, Rohru, Rampur, southern Kullu, central Palampur, Bharmaur, Chamba and Churah areas. These soils are rich in iron and carbon but lack salts and other mineral constituents. Not suitable for agriculture these are given to pastures and meadows. Presently these are increasingly being used for horticulture.

(v) *Dry Hill Soil Zone*

These soils are found in Lahul and Spiti, Kinnaur, northern Kullu and Pangi where monsoonal rainfall is small. These are high textured soils with a variable fertility. Organic status is almost low. These are infertile and are thus suitable for growth of grasses, pastures and shrubs.

On the whole, the soils in the region are young and thin and depth in them occures in the valleys or on gently inclined hill slopes. Owing to rugged topography the profiles are channery: diffuse boundaries between the genetic horizons indicate their skeletal character. Agricultural occupance, human settlements, and the distribution of cultivable soils are found co-terminus all over the State. The soils are partly irrigated and munured or supplied with full irrigation on relatively levelled tracts consisting of sandy or clay loams. The patches of valley soils are considered to be the best in trans-Pir Panjal area. With considerable local variations, away from the valley area it becomes stony and gravelly towards the upper-most sections of stream courses. In the inside glens of Spiti, the soil is pebbly and gravelly as if it were under water for long long time.

Religious Landscape

This land presents features of peculiar interest to a student of religion and sociology. In the plains of Punjab Brahmanism or Hinduism has always remained weaker than in other parts of India. Coming into contact with other faiths and the people of diverse nationalities, the religion and the social mores of the people naturally underwent a metamorphosis. In this hilly region, though next door to Punjab, the Hindu religion and the caste system, to which it has given birth, have remained free in an unusual degree from external influences. The isolated location and the inaccessibility of the region is primarily the reason why it escaped any onslaught on the social milieu of the people. The people are almost exclusively Hindus, curiously strict as regards some and lax as regards other ordinances of the religion. 'The ethnical character of the tract is due to its inaccessibility and remoteness from the lines which foreign inroads into India have always taken' explains Ibbetson, Sir Denzil in the Census report for Punjab, 1883. Continuing he observes: 'It is here then that we might expect to find caste existing most nearly in the same state as that in which the first Muhammadan invaders found it when they entered Punjab. But it is difficult to say with certainty that here the Brahman and the Kshtriya occupy positions most nearly resembling those assigned to them by Manu'. Concluding he sums up: 'One is almost tempted to believe that the type of Hindu society still found in this tract preserves an even more archaic organization than anything described by Manu.' In short, the kind of religion and the nature of the caste system prevalent here may be considered to represent the primitive and archaic form somewhat deteriorated by decay from within. It is certainly not the Hinduism of the Vedas. It is, on the other hand, religion of the masses with paraphernalia of the worship of natural forces and objects, trees and animals; abstract beings such as ancestors, ghosts, spirits, hob-goblins, witches, heroes and heroines. The various aspects of Nature and the manifestations of physical forces allotted to a multitude of gods and goddesses, in numerous forms and with various names, are worshipped to propitiate them or to ask for boons according as these are malevolent or benevolent in nature. Reverence of the Brahman, strict adherence to caste rules and meticulous observance of ceremonial rituals, abstention from ceremonial pollution are the usual features of the religion of these people loosened somewhat with the entry of the modern era. Animal sacrifice is a characteristic of their rituals, through not at a scale as in days of yore. Religion 'crusted, and eroded over ages', in short, plays a vital role in the life of these people.

Population—Decadal Variation

The State has an area of 55,673 square kilometres, more than the area of any one of the two neighbouring States of Punjab and Haryana. Its population rose by 8,90,059 persons during 1981-91 decade to stand at 5,170,877 on 1st March, sun-rise, 1991.[15] In the past it has been :

Table 1.1: Decadal Variation in Population in Himachal Pradesh

Year	Population	Decennial growth rate %	Females per '000 males	Density per sq. km.
1901	1920294	-	884	34
1911	1896944	(-) 1.22	889	34
1921	1928206	(+) 1.65	890	35
1931	2029113	(+) 5.23	897	36
1941	2263245	(+) 11.54	890	41
1951	2385981	(+) 5.42	912	43
1961	2812463	(+) 17.87	938	51
1971	3460434	(+) 23.04	958	62
1981	4280818	(+) 23.71	973	77
1991	5170877	(+) 20.79	976	93

Source: *Statistical Outline, Himachal Pradesh,* 1994

From the Table it is observed that the population of Himachal Pradesh increased from 1.92 million in 1901 to 2.02 million in 1931 giving a marginal increase of barely one lakh persons. But for the negative growth rate (-1.22 per cent) in 1911 attributed to natural calamities such as Kangra earth quake of 1905 which took a heavy toll of 20,000 human lives as also the epidemics, the curve has been gentle. From 1941 onwards, however, the graph shows a phenomenal rise from as low as +5.4 per cent in 1941-51 to as high as 23.71 per cent in 1971-81. During the last decade (1981-91) it has though dipped a bit to stabilise at +20.79 per cent obviously due to family planning effort. On the whole the population which was barely 1,920,294 in 1901 has sky-rocketed to 5,170,877. It is a mind-boggling increase of almost 270 per cent. Even if territorial accretions of 1966 are taken into account the increase is still far from comforting.

In this context, it would be of interest to bear in mind the birth and death rates as well. *Sample Registration Bulletin* (Vol. xxvi, No. 1, June, 1992) came out with the following estimates:

Table 1.2: Birth and Death Rates in Himachal Pradesh

Year	Birth rate		Death rate	
	India	H. P.	India	H. P.
1986	32.6	30.6	11.1	8.7
1987	32.2	30.8	10.9	8.5
1988	31.5	32.2	11.0	9.6
1989	30.6	27.7	10.3	8.7
1990	30.2	27.4	9.7	8.5

During 1901-11, the districts of Kangra, Hamirpur, Una, Shimla and Solan recorded negative growth of population. In Solan district the population went down by 20.74 per cent. During 1911-21, Kullu, Lahul and Spiti and Kinnaur districts showed negative growth of population. Again during 1921-31 Solan district recorded negative growth rate by 5.71 per cent. From 1931 onwards through there is considerable variation in the decadal growth yet all the districts added positive growth of population uptil 1981. During 1951-61, Lahul and Spiti district with 54.40 per cent recorded a phenomenal increase and during 1961-71 Mandi district earned the dubious distinction of having the highest growth rate of 34.07 per cent.

Spatial Distribution

There is distinct clustering of population in the valleys: areas of harsh climate and steep inclines are thinly populated. The high and rugged mountain ranges with snow-capped pinnacles and forest-clad slopes are practically uninhabited. Of the twelve district in the State, Hamirpur continues to have the highest density of population (330) distantly followed by Bilaspur (253), Una (246), Kangra (205) and not so close by Mandi and Solan (both 197) persons per square kilometre. It proves the statement that 'like mineral veins in a rock, valleys are rich in population element.[16] Where the country is inhospitable, it is sparsely populated as in the case of Kullu (55) and Chamba (60) districts. The trans-Himalayan tracts of Lahul and Spiti and Kinnaur carry very little population as they are semi-arid highland zones, the former maintaining status *quo ante* with two persons per sq. km. as in 1971, and Kinnaur a little better at 11 person as compared to 8 persons per sq. km. in 1971.

Rural-Urban Composition

Himachal Pradesh being pre-dominantly a hilly State, 91.31% of its population is rural, living in 16,997 inhabited villages: the number of urbanites concentrated in 58 towns is 449,196, in other words, barely 8.69% of the total population. Lahul and Spiti and Kinnaur districts have 100% rural population. Of the other districts, Kangra has the highest number of ruralites (1,114,723) and Kullu district the least (281,421). Shimla district has the distinction of highest urban population of 126,132 of which Shimla Municipal Corporation alone accounts for 82,054 persons. The least urban population inhabits the Bilaspur district: 10,609 of the total 16,735 reside in Bilaspur town.

Occupational Structure

According to 1991 Census the main workers constitute 34.41 and the marginal workers 8.42 per cent of the total population. Of both 43.57% belong to rural areas and 34.98% to cities and towns. Incidentally more than half of the total population, to be exact 57.17%, is the non-working segment. Of the main workers 63.25% are cultivators and as few as 3.30%, the agricultural labourers, of whom about one-third are accounted for in Kangra district alone. Of the remaining 33.45%, only 1.43 per cent are engaged in household industries and the remaining 32.02% in other activities. Interestingly almost as many workers are engaged in trade and commerce (78,253) as are in construction activities (86,246). Exactly half of the construction workers are those engaged in forestry, fishing, hunting, horticulture and live-stock rearing (43,957). Shorn of those engaged in agriculture related activities, other occupations show a meagre percentage. This is mainly due to the fact that economically the State is under-developed and secondary and tertiary sectors are poorly developed.

Sex-Ratio

Sex ratio in Himachal Pradesh presents a very interesting study. The following Table reveals that female population in the State is fast narrowing the gap with male population.

Table 1.3: Sex ratio

Year	Sex-ratio Per '000 males	Year	Sex-ratio per '000 males
1901	885	1911	904
1921	902	1931	906
1941	897	1951	915
1961	923	1971	958
1981	988	-	-

Now (1991) there are 976 females per 1,000 males for the State as a whole though for rural areas the figure is better at 990. As per the past trend the female population is on the increase and, in fact in some districts, it has actually overtaken the male population. For example in the district of Hamirpur for every thousand males it is 1,105; in Kangra, 1,024; in Una 1,017; in Mandi 1,013 and in Bilaspur 1,002. Polyandrous Lahul and Spiti has the lowest ratio of 817. In the neighbouring Kinnaur it is slightly higher at 856 women per 1,000 males.

Literacy

It may be recalled that as per 1971 Census, the State had 31.96 per cent literaté population compared to the national average of 29.45 per cent. During 1961-71, literacy growth rate at 84.92 per cent was the highest in the country. During 1971-81 the decadal growth rate dropped to 60.71 per cent though the overall State literacy percentage rose to 41.94 as against the national average of 34.80 per cent. In 1991 the literacy rate jumped from 51.17 per cent in 1981 to 63.86 for total population (75.36 for males and 52.13 for females). In this decade again the rate is higher than All-India percentage. The highest rise has been recorded in Hamirpur district (74.88%) and the lowest in Chamba (44.70%). The districts of Mandi (62.74%), Kullu (54.82%), Lahul and Spiti (56.82%), Solan (63.38%), Sirmur (51.62%) and Kinnaur (58.36%) have lagged behind the State average. The female literacy rate is below the State average in the districts of Kullu, Lahul and Spiti, Shimla, Solan, Sirmur, Kinnaur and Mandi.

Racial Profile

The geographical entity itself would have had no meaning but for the cultural, racial, and linguistic affinity among the people of the State. By and large the people wear Aryan features. Khasas are said to be of Aryan stock and include the high caste groups like Brahmans and Rajputs. The other major ancestral stock takes lineage from the indigenous people of the hills known as *Domes*. They constitute low caste groups, such as, blacksmith, carpenter, shoe-maker, musician, weaver, tailor, basket-maker, etc. 'In the hills and in the *Dun*' writes Walton, 'they (*Domes*) comprise all classes who do menial and more or less degrading duties such as are performed by separate occupational castes in the plains. They are a depressed race, seldom cultivate and practically never own land.'[17] The scheduled castes comprising a number of sub-castes form 25.34 per cent of the State's population. In the caste-ridden society, Brahman forms 12 per cent and is found disseminated all through the State. In several regions he forms a well defined agricultural class, distinct from the Brahman who performs sacerdotal functions as a profession as also from other secular castes. The minor castes of Ghirath and Jat, among the agriculturists, and Khatri, Sood and Mahajan among the traditional business communities constitute nearly 7 per cent of the population: Rajputs of various grades constitute the largest chunk. Because of the ascendancy of this caste, the region 'might also be called ethnographically the Rajputana of the Punjab as it has been called its Switzerland from the physical characteristics.' (Glossary of the Tribes and Castes, 1883).

In a predominantly Hindu population there is sprinkling of Muslims (1.72% -1.63 % in 1981), Christians (0.90%) Sikhs (1.01%-1.22% in 1981) and Buddhists (1.24%). These minority communities have specific centres of concentration. Over 70% of the Muslims are found in Chamba (6.29%), Kangra (1.00%), Una (2.28%), Bilaspur (1.48%), Sirmur (5.10%) and Solan (1.74%) district. The area along Indo-Tibetan contact zone comprising Kinnaur and Lahul and Spiti districts is home to 60 per cent of the Buddhists and another 33 per cent live in small pockets in the districts of Chamba, Kangra, Kullu, and Sirmur. Over 90 per cent of the Sikhs are settled in the towns of Kangra, Mandi, Shimla and Paonta with Una and Nalagarh having them in rural areas as well. And of every five Christians, three live in the towns of Shimla, Kangra, Solan and Chamba districts.

In absolute terms the population of Scheduled Castes (56 in number) and Scheduled Tribes notified for the State with some area restrictions in case of Gaddi and Gujars, has gone up considerably. Returned at 1,310,296 persons (as compared to 1,053,958 in 1981) the Scheduled Castes population in 1991 stands at 25.34 per cent of the total population. During the preceding decade (1971-81) their population had registered a much higher growth rate of 36.95 per cent: the State's growth rate was 23.71 per cent only. The proportion of the Scheduled Castes to total population has risen from 24.64 per cent in 1981 to 25.34 per cent in the 1991Census: the highest proportion reported from Solan district (31.27%) closely followed by Sirmaur district (30.18%). The other districts having proportion above the State average are Mandi (28.98%), Kullu (28.93%), Shimla (27.13%), Kinnaur (26.87%) and Bilaspur (25.82%). The lowest proportion of 7.11% has been reported from Lahul and Spiti district. As high as 94.64 per cent of them live in villages and remaining 6.33 per cent constitute the urban component: highest (9.52%) returned from the urban areas of Shimla district. Their sex ratio also showed a rising trend; from 950 in 1971 to 959 per '000 males in 1981. During the same period, the literacy rate too went up by +12.68 per cent, unhappily less for women (+10.89%) than for males (+14.56%).

Another 4.22 per cent of the population are the Scheduled Tribes constituting the largest single concentration in the West Himalaya. The Scheduled Tribes chiefly inhabit the inner trans-Pir Panjal zone in Kinnaur, Lahul and Spiti and Pangi (Chamba district). The only exception is of Bharmour sub-division of Chamba district. Known after these tracts these hill tribes are Gaddis, Kinnars, Lahaulis, and Pangwals. Almost 75 per cent of these tribals follow Hindu beliefs or a faith which is harmonious blend of Hindu-Buddhist practices.

The notified Scheduled Tribes in Himachal Pradesh are eight in number, *viz;*

1. Bhot, Bodh;
2. Gaddi (excluding the territories specified in sub-section (1) section 5 of the Punjab Re-organization Act, 1966, other than the Lahul and Spiti district.)[18];
3. Gujar (excluding the territories specified in sub-section (1) of section 5 of the Punjab Re-organization Act, 1966);
4. Jad, Lamba, Khampa;
5. Kanaura, Kinnara;
6. Lahaula;
7. Pangwala; and
8. Swangla.

As per the 1991 Census their combined population forms 4.22 per cent of the total population of the State: in 1981 this percentage was 4.61 and still earlier in 1971 marginally less at 4.09. The Chamba district has the largest Scheduled Tribes population of 111,509 persons (1981-95, 726 and 1971 -67,852): Kinnaur district ranking second with 39,609 persons (1981- 44,583) followed by Lahul & Spiti with 24,088 (1981-23,766). Una is once again at the tail end with only 55 persons belonging to Scheduled tribes enumerated in the whole of that district. Sex ratio among them also shows some variation. In 1971 there was one woman for every man; in 1981 however, the figure came down to 978 (State average 973) per one thousand males. Literacy rate which stood at 15.89 per cent in 1971 went up by +10.04 per cent to record at 25.93 in 1981. Here again the women lagged far behind registering only +7.29 per cent increase whereas for males the corresponding figure was +12.50 per cent. According to 1991 Census data the literacy rate for Scheduled castes (53.20%) and Scheduled tribes (47.09%) is far low than the literacy rate for general population (63.86%). At the district level the highest literacy rate among Schedule castes has been reported from Hamirpur (68.51%) and the lowest from Chamba (36.88%). It would be interesting to note that in case of Scheduled Tribes, the literacy rate in the districts of Kangra (78.88%), Hamirpur (96.19%), Una (90.57%), Kullu (68.21%) and Kinnaur (59.03%) has surpassed the general literacy rate of these districts.

There are two kinds of Gujars, *viz.,* the resident Gujar, who owns fields and a house, and pastures his herd in the neighbouring waste, and the *ban* or forest Gujar, who has no land or fixed home and moves with his herd, spending his summer in a shed on the high ranges and winters in the woody parts of the lower hills. The nomadic Gujars are exclusively a pastoral tribe. They live in the skirts of the forests and maintain their existence by the sale of milk, ghee and other produce of their herds. Their wealth consists of buffaloes, as that of the Gaddis consists chiefly of sheep and goats. They are pre-dominantly Muslim by faith: Hindu Gujars found mostly in the districts of Mandi, Kangra, Sirmour, Solan and Bilaspur have now settled down and taken to farming. They donot have any identity marker. Most conservative, the Muslim *ban* Gujars continue to stick to the traditional nomadic life exhibiting callous indifference to settle permanently and join the main stream.

Cultural Mosaic

The various cultural streams which poured into the region from different directions have created a delightful whirlpool of social life. Fortunately the region was only partially sanskritized with the result that the folk culture remains the dominant theme. The physical setting of the mountainous region has played a significant role in the making of its cultural environment. And so has the community life. Group inter-action amongst numerous classes of people has left indelible imprint on the cultural landscape. In addition, the Nature and the tract's situation along the cultural Indo-Tibetan zone, its physical isolation from the outside world, all have allowed the prevailing religious beliefs a far greater scope to influence the cultural mosaic. Historically there has been no common source of different ethnic groups in the State. The caste structure of the Hindu society still retains its peculiar characteristics.

The geographical isolation and the consequential laxity in the purity of caste has enleashed both the divisive and cohesive forces and it is their inter-play which has tended to produce the present composite *pahari* culture.

The distant Himalayas, capped with snow, convey an impression of eternity. They have a quiet splendour and a quality of timelessness that makes the activities of man seem irrelevant and trivial. Living in tranquillity in the harshness of long winter months and toughness of the topography has perhaps given the people a strange blend of humility, sensitivity and hardiness to survive against heavy odds. They are happy and joyous people, who love to sing and dance. Their folk lore is full of songs of chivalry, love, of victory, of good over evil, of a free and fearless society where Lord Shiva and his consort Parvati reign supreme. They share a variety of folk dances accompanied by sweet musical notes. Their most popular dance form is *nati.*

Men and women, old and young, all love fairs and festivals. Almost every village has its own fair. Fairs and festivals are generally held in honour of the local gods and goddesses. Of some, origin can be traced to religious or otherwise holy or sacred concept or commemoration. Lavi fair is perhaps the only fair which is not connected with any legend or religious belief. It is an economic or trade fair as are the Nalwar fairs of Sundernagar (Mandi) and of Bilaspur comparatively of recent origin.

The very name of Himachal Pradesh evokes visions of snow and sunshine and of gods and goddesses. Verily it is 'dev bhoomi', and God surely must be residing here where even man feels he is in heaven. Every village has its distinctive *deo* or *devi* apart from the universal deity in the form of Durga, Kali, Chaturbhuja, Chamunda, Maha Kali or Shiva linga symbolising the Shiva-Shakti cult.

Linguistically too the State has some distinctive features. There are as many dialects as, once in the past, there were princely states. Encyclopedia Britanica puts the number at about 60. Uniformity has persuaded linguists to group these dialects as 'western Pahari'. Dr. Grierson enumerated *Jaunsari, Sirmuri, Baghati, Kiunthali, Satluj group, Kulvi,*

Mandiali, Chambiali and *bhadrawahi* belonging to western Pahari group. Kangri also is a dialect of the area. According to well-known authorities they have their origin in Sanskrit and Prakrit.

Himachal Pradesh reminds one of its ancient heritage which has survived mostly in the form of temple architecture, wood carvings, stone and metal sculptures and paintings. Khasa style is the earliest known form. It is based on wood. The earliest example is found on the copper and silver coins of Audumbras (2nd century B.C.) Vast number of temples scattered all over the middle belt of Himachal Himalayas are in *deodar* wood. The pent roof temples are the most ancient. Pyramidical temples are mostly found in the Jubbal valley. The pagoda style can be seen in Mandi, Kullu, Shimla Hills and Kinnaur. The fourth style, fusion of pent and pagoda styles, is represented in the temples of Vahana Mahadev and Dhaneshwari Devi in outer Seraj. The earliest specimen of the Nagara design is found in the monolithic temples of Masroor in Kangra district and the Mani Mahesh temple in Bharmour.

The kind of religion and nature of the caste system as presently obtains in the State presents a glimpse of the successive phases of their primitive nature and archaic form. Inspite of exotic influences, the religio-social structure still exposes the fossils and remnants of an ancient social and cultural fabric of the society. The alpine regions lying in the lap of higher Himalaya and surrounded by lofty ranges isolating them from one another as also from the rest of the State exhibit a unique picture of the tribal cultural life. Verily no other State in India is endowed with such a diversity of cultural patterns. The legendary lands of Kullu, Kinnaur, Lahul and Spiti with traces of Bonpaism and Tibetan Lamaism stand out as distinct cultural entities. The Brahman, the Rajput, the Kanet, the Ghirath, the Dum, the Koli, the Dagi, all with distinctive customs and culture form a most bewitching cultural mosaic.

Himachal Pradesh is a small world in itself, culturally diverse yet smelling of the same soil and drawing inspiration from a common past history; effervescent, seething with latent human energy, in short, a crucible of great potentialities.

Notes and References

1. B.B. Lal: Palaeoliths from the Beas and Bangana Valley Punjab; *Science India*, Vol. XIII.

2. Joshi, R.V.: Stone Age-Environment and Cultural Sequence in the Kangra Valley, Himachal Pradesh in V.C. Ohri's *Pre-History of Himachal Pradesh*, 1979.

3. Kayastha, S.L.: *The Himalayan Beas Basin: A Study in the Habitat, Economic and Society*; Varanasi, 1964.

4. Singh Mian Goverdhan: *Pre-History and Proto-History in Himachal—Past, Present and Future*; H.P. University, 1975.

5. Cunningham, Sir Alexander: *Ancient Geography of India*, 1924.

6. Kangra Sevak Sabha: 'Glimpses from the Past'—*Annual Number*, K.S.S.; Delhi, 1953.

7. Punjab Government: *Gazetteer of the Kangra District, Pt. I, Kangra, 1883-84*; Reprint New Delhi, 1994.

8. Punjab Government: *Punjab District Gazetteer, Vol. VIII A-Simla District Part A, 1904*; Lahore, 1904.

9. Verma, V.: *The Emergence of Himachal Pradesh*; Chapter 14; New Delhi, 1995.

10. Handa, O.C.: *Textile, Costumes and Ornaments of the Western Himalaya*; New Delhi, 1998.

11. Punjab Government: *Gazetteer of the Kangra District op. cit.*

12. Wadia, D.N.: *Geology of India*; London, 1949.

13. Singh, R.L. (Ed.): *India—A Regional Geography*; Varanasi, 1971.

14. Raychaudhri, S.P.: *Land and Soil*; NBTI, India, Delhi, 1966.

15. Break-up according to 1991 Census:

	Total	Rural	Urban	Literacy Ratio	Sex Ratio	S.C. Population	S.T. Population
Chamba	393,286	363,397	29,889	44.70	949	77,667	111,509
Kangra	1,174,072	1,114,723	59,349	70.57	1,024	248,498	1,620
Hamirpur	369,128	346,442	22,686	74.88	1,105	87,394	223
Una	378,269	345,997	32,272	70.91	1,017	84,978	55
Bilaspur	295,387	278,652	16,735	67.17	1,002	76,281	7,983
Mandi	776,372	720,603	55,769	62.74	1,013	224,998	9,417
Kullu	302,432	281,421	21,011	54.82	920	87,489	10,914
Lahul & Spiti	31,294	31,294	-	56.82	817	2,224	24,088
Shimla	617,404	491,272	126,132	64.61	894	167,482	4,369

(Contd...)

	Total	Rural	Urban	Literacy Ratio	Sex Ratio	S.C. Population	S.T.Population
Solan	382,268	334,989	47,279	63.30	909	119,527	2,449
Sirmur	379,695	341,621	38,074	51.62	897	114,605	6,113
Kinnaur	71,270	71,270	-	58.36	856	19,153	39,609
Himachal Pradesh	**5,170,877**	**4,721,681**	**449,196**	**63.86**	**976**	**1,310,296**	**218,349**

16. Kayastha, S.L.: 'Demographic Features of the Himalayan Beas Basin'; *N.G.J.I; II, 1.,* (March '56).

17. Walton, H.G.: *District Gazetteer of United Province; of Agra and Oudh*; Allahabad, 1911.

18. For detailed study of Gaddi, Pangwal and Bodh tribes the author's following books may be consulted with advantage:

   (i) *Gaddis of Dhauladhar—A Transhumant Tribe of the Himalaya*; New Delhi, 1996.

   (ii) *Pangi—A Tribal Habitat in Mid-Himalaya*; New Delhi, 1997.

   (iii) *Spiti —A Buddhist Land in Western Himalaya*; New Delhi, 1997.

2

*Gujars—History and Origin

Wedded to herding buffaloes and migrating from summer to winter pastures and vice-versa, year after year, the Muslim Gujars in Himachal Pradesh lead a nomadic life. From time immemorial they have been living in this fashion, far removed from the modern civilization, nurturing a distinct social and cultural mosaic of their own. Unlike their Hindu brethren in the plains as also in Himachal Pradesh, who, over ages have taken up cultivation as their main source of livlihood and given up nomadism in favour of a sedentary life, they are exclusively a pastoral tribe evincing little interest in a settled life and any vocation other than dairy farming. They have no living tradition of their origin in the distant past. What they, however, do recall is that their forefathers migrated to this area from the adjoining territory of Kishtwar in Jammu and Kashmir. Though differing in their pet theories and varying approaches, the historians are united on one point. All of them hold that the present-day Gujars belong to Gurjara race, which rode high in the political firmament of the country from about sixth century to the end of the thirteenth century.

Very little material is available to construct a reliable history of second half of the sixth century A.D. This much, however, is beyond doubt that after the golden age of the Gupta empire, which had lasted from 370 to 455 A.D., the Hunas poured into India in successive waves. These white Hunas, however, held a comparatively short-lived supremacy over Northern India. Between 563 and 567 A.D. the Turkish

* 'In the mountains ..... throughout the hill country ... and also in the hills of Kashmir .... they are called 'Gujurs' (not Gujar or Gujar)'. G.A. Grierson's *Linguistic Survey of India* (Vol. IX Part IV).

tribes in alliance with the Persian King destroyed them and extended their dominion over all the countries once included in the Huna empire.[1] Soon after the Hunas, historians hold, came the Gurjaras, who may indeed have come along with them, though they are not heard of until near the end of the sixth century when they shine into prominence. Apparently taking advantage of the waning Gupta empire, they succeeded in establishing their political dominance. So powerful did these Gurjaras, or Gujars became that no fewer than four tracts of the country received their name after them. In modern geography these are the districts of Gujrat and Gujranwala in Pakistan, and the State of Gujrat in India. In addition to these three tracts Al-Biruni (971-1,039 A.D.) mentions Guzarat situated somewhere in northern Rajputana. The district of Saharanpur (Uttar Pradesh) was also called Gujarat in the eighteenth century and one of the northern districts of Gwalior is still called Gujargarh. These name-places indicate that the Gurjaras had quite a large number of settlements spread over the length and breadth of the country. This inference is further corroborated by the present distribution of the Gujars. They are fairly numerous in the Western Himalaya, Jammu and Kashmir and Himachal Pradesh, the Punjab, the Uttar Pradesh and the Western Rajputana and are also found in the hill country beyond the Sindhu.

Origin-different Theories

The origin of the Gurjaras is a subject of keen controversy. They are identified by General Cunningham[2] with the Kushan, or Yuchi alias Touchari, a tribe of Eastern Tartars. About a century before Christ their chief conquered Kabul and the Peshwar country while his son Hima Kadphises extended his sway over the whole of the upper Punjab and along the banks of the Yamuna as far down as Mathura and the Vindhyas. His successor, the no less familiar king Kanishka, the first Buddhist Indo-Scythian prince, annexed Kashmir to the Tochari kingdom. Probably about the beginning of the third century A.D. the invasion of the White Huns recalled the last king of the united Yuchi (Great Yuchi and Kator or little Yuchi) to the west. Before the end of the third century a portion of the Gujars had begun to move southward down the Indus, and were shortly afterwards separated from their northern brethren by another Indo-Scythian wave from the north. In the middle of the fifth century there was a Gujar kingdom in south-western Rajputana, whence they were driven by the Balas into Gujrat and about the end of ninth century, Ala Khana, the Gujar king of Jammu, ceded the Gujar-*des*, corresponding very nearly with the Gujrat district (now in Pakistan) to the king of Kashmir.

The theory of Cunningham, claiming Gujars to be connected with the Yuchi tribe of Central Asia is rejected by Risley[3] on the ground that the Yuchi was almost certainly of the brachycephlic type, while the Gujars, he claims, are dolichocephalic. He includes them in what he calls, the 'Indo-Aryan Branch'. This concept has been supported by Crooke, W.[4], who calls them as a' fairly typical Indo-Aryan' race.

In the opinion of Smith, V., Gujars or Gurjaras formed a branch of the White Hunas, who invaded India in the fifth and sixth centuries. According to him:[5]

> The earliest foreign immigration within the limits of the historical period which can be verified is that of the Sakas in the second century B.C.; and the next is that of the Yueh-chi and the Kushanas in the first century A.D...... The third recorded great irruption of foreign barbarians occurred during the fifth century and the early part of the sixth. There are indications that the immigration from Central Asia continued during the third century, but, if it did, no distinct record of the event has been preserved, and, so far as positive knowledge goes, only three certain irruptions of foreigners on a large scale through the northern and north-western passes can be proved to have taken place within the historical period anterior to the Muhammadan invasions of the tenth and eleventh centuries.

The third irruption of the Hunas or White Hunas, of which, according to him, Gurjaras was an important element, made their principal permanent settlements in the

Punjab and Rajputana tracts. And in early mediaeval times
the Gurjara kingdoms acquired a prominent position on the
political map of India. Of the Gurjara empire, king Bhoja
(840-890 A.D.), his predecessors and successors belonged to
the well-known clan Pratihara (Parihar), a Rajput branch of
the Gurjara or Gujar stock.

Late Sir J. Campbell, on his part, has identified the Gujars
with the Khazar tribe of Central Asia. According to him "the
Gujaras seem to have formed part of the great horde of which
the Juan-Juan or Avars, and the Ephthalites, Yetas or White
Hunas were leading elements."[6] Proceeding further he asks
the question and provides the answer thus:

> The question remains: How far does the arrival of
> the Gurjara in India, during the early sixth century,
> agree with what is known of the history of Khazar?
> The name Khazar appears under the following
> forms: Among Chinese as Kosa, among Russians
> as Khwalisses, among Byzantines as Chozars or
> Chazars, among Armenians as Khazirs and among
> Arabs as Khozar. Other variations come closer to
> Gujara. These are Gazar, the form Kazar takes to
> the north of the sea of Asof; Ghysar, the name for
> Khazars who have become Jews; and Ghusar, the
> form of Khazar in use among the Lesghians of the
> Caucasus. Howarth and the writer in the
> *Encyclopaedia Britannica* follow Klaproth in holding
> that the Khazars are the same as the white Hunas.

The Khazars included two distinct elements, a fair or
Ak-Khazar, the Akatziroi or Khazaroi of Byzantine historians,
and a dark or Kara Khazar. The former was fair skinned,
black-haired, and beautiful and the Kara Khazar, short and
ugly. He was the Ughrian nomad of the steppes, who formed
the rank and file of the army. A trace both of the beautiful
and coarse clans seems to survive in the complimentary
Marwar proverb, 'Handsome as a Huna' and in the abusive
Gujrat proverb, 'Yellow and short as a Hun's beard.' Campbell
concludes that under its Hindu form Gurjara, Khazar
appears to have become the name by which the great bulk
of the sixth century horde was known, and that the Sesodia

or Gahlot Rajputs, the most illustrious of all the clans, were of Gujar stock, as well as the Parihar, Chauhan, and Chalukya or Solanki, three of the *agnikula* clans.

Relating the origin of the Gujars, the *Glossary of the Tribes and Castes of the Punjab and NWFP* [7] (Vol. II) records:

> According to Dr. Rudolf Hoernle the Tomaras (the modern Tunwar Rajputs) were a clan of the Gurjaras, and indeed their imperial or ruling clan. The Pehowa (Pehoa in the Karnal district) inscription records of a Tomara family that it was descended from a raja, Jaula, whose name recalls that of the Shahi Javavla or Jahula and of the maharaja, Toranmana Shahi Jauvla of the Kura inscription. Dr. Hoernle thinks it probable that the Kachhwahas and Parihars, like the Tomaras, were all clans or division of a Javula tribe claiming descent from Toramana, king of the white Huns or Ephthalites. Mr. Bhandarkar has shown that the Solankis (Chaulakyas), Parihars (Pratiharas), Parmars (Paramaras) and Chauhans (Chahumanas or Chahuvanas), the four so-called clans of Rajputs, were originally divisions of the Gurjaras, and to these Dr. Hoernle would thus add the Tomaras and Kachhwahas. The exact ethnic relation of the Gurjaras to the Huns is still very obscure, but as a working hypothesis Dr. Hoernle thinks that in the earlier part of the 6th century A.D. a great invasion of Central Asiatic peoples, Huns, Gurjaras and others, whose exact interrelation we do not know, took place. The first onset carried them as far as Gwalior, but it was checked by the emperor of Kanauj, and the main portion of these foreign hordes settled in the Rajputana and the Punjab, while the Chaulakyas turned South. In the north the invaders fused with the natives of the country and in the middle of the 7th century the Parihars emerged, an upgrowth followed by the Parmars, Chauhans and imperial Gurjaras about 750 A.D. About 840 the Gurjara empire, with its capital at

Kanauj, embraced nearly the whole of northern India, under Bhoja I, but after his death it declined.

According to yet another school of thought they migrated[8] from Georgia, a country situated between the Black sea and the Caspian sea in Russia. In Persian it is called Gurjarstan, from which the term Gujar is said to have been derived. It would be interesting to refer to the ethnological study of Gujars by Prof. Georgi Chogoshrill of the Georgian Academy of Sciences (1967) which has highlighted 'remarkable similarities' between the Georgians and the Gujars. In the view of Prof. Levan Maruashill of the Georgian Institute of Geography, 'there is enough evidence to sustain a case for a thorough study to find out when the Georgians first started moving to India.'

In the opinion of Arab geographers, Gujars were the inhabitants of Juzr,[9] which Al-Idisi quoting Ibn Khordadbeh mentions as the hereditary title of the king as also the name of a country.

Legend is that the Gujars are descendants[10] of Prophet Ishaque, to be precise, the progeny and followers of his elder son, Hazrat Ash, who was superseded to the *khilafat* (prophet-hood) by his younger brother, Hazrat Yakub. The story goes that on being denied the right of succession, Ash overcome by despair left his home and went into the forest. There Allah came to him in a vision, consoled him and told him to have faith in His Word and lead a simple and sinless life. Ever since his descendants and followers, the present-day Gujars, lead a simple life wandering in the forests in the belief that they are thus nearer to God. It is a myth: historically it has no substance. Yet another fanciful version is that their name comes from *gua-charana* meaning 'to graze cattle'. An equally imaginative origin is the Hindi word, *gajar* (carrot) from the mistaken belief that the Gujars fed their cattle on carrots.

The Scythian[11] origin of the Gurjaras, accepted as an historical fact has been maintained on three main grounds, namely, *(i)* the custom of the *Karao;*

(ii) the worship of snakes; and

(iii) the identification of proper names.

The first argument has no legs to stand on because the marriage of the elder brother's widow was a Hindu custom legalised by Manu's code, and though it was prohibited to the higher castes by the code of Parasara, it is still practised by all the lower castes, and is not, nor ever has been, confined to the Gujars only. The second ground is like-wise worth nothing, because snakes are worshipped all over India by all castes alike. The third argument (identification of proper names) is ingenious, but far from convincing. The term Gujar is merely a variant of *gochar* or cattle-grazer. Again, as this so-called Scythian tribe is in physical characteristics precisely similar to the rest of the Indian population, it is vain to expect one to believe that the Gujars are of an alien ethnical stock. 'Moreover, the pastoral castes are the necessary intermediate link between the hunting and the agricultural; and this fact alone, unless we are to discredit the analogies of history and the conclusions of science, is sufficient to prove that they are not of foreign but of indigenous blood."[12]

The theory of foreign origin of the Gurjaras is contested strenuously by many distinguished men of learning. Krishnaswami Iyengar, one of the many historians of the same view, states:[13]

> I do believe that the immigration of the Gurjaras is not such a settled fact of history for deductive applications. I did my best to examine the materials on which the theory of immigration was based and I submit that in view of all the evidence that has been forthcoming of recent years, the theory of immigration is unsustainable..............
>
> I venture, therefore to submit that there is no determinative piece of evidence to prove that the word 'Gurjara' was used to indicate the race of the person denominated; or that the person denominated was of foreign origin.

Gurjara—A Country or a Race

Were Gurjaras a tribe or does the word as used in the primary sense indicative of a home land? In K.M. Munshi's[14] strongly held opinion, Gurjara, was primarily the name of a country, whose inhabitants were naturally known as Gurjaras. It has been suggested that the various geographical units now called Gujrat (or allied names) were originally parts of a large homogeneous country named Gurjaradesa under the political authority of its own kings, and while isolated fragments of it have retained the old names, others have lost it.

Gurjaras are not mentioned in the *Mahabharata* nor in the *Vishnu, Bhagavata* or *Markandeya Purana*. In fact the earliest known reference to them occurs in the *Sriharshacharita*, a work of the early part of the seventh century. In this work Bana describes[15] Prabhakaravardhana, the father of Harshavardhana, as 'the lion to the deer which is the Huna, the dangerous fever of Sindhuraja, the one who kept the Gurjara awake, the fell disease to the elephant of Gandhara, the thief of the expanse of Lata, the axe to the creeper of the sovereignty of Malava'. This passage has often been relied upon to show the close connection between the Hunas and the Gujraras, but according to Munshi, it reads otherwise. According to him, of the proper nouns used by Bana only one, namely 'Huna' indicates a tribe and the rest are undisputedly the names of countries or of the king of Sindhu country. To fortify this position, Munshi has additionally relied on the Aihole inscription of Pulakesi II composed shortly after *Harishacharita* as also on an inscription of A.D. 739 describing conquest of the Arabs over different kings as also on a few more examples of similar nature.

This view has not, however, met with general acceptance. For while there is no evidence that the mighty empire of the Pratiharas had a common geographical name and a homogeneous character as distinguished from the rest of India, several parts of it have retained distinct names throughout the duration of that empire and even later. The various localities clearly associated in old times with the name Gurjara, and the present distribution of the people called Gujars, undoubtedly favour the view that the term primarily denoted a people, and the countries derived their names from them. But though we can be more or less sure that the Gurjaras were originally the name of a people, there is no definite evidence that they were foreigners and came to India in a historical time in the wake of Hunas, the Kushanas or other foreign hordes.

The Gurjaras were in the main a pastoral people, but had their chiefs and fighting men. When the tribe rose to power, the latter were treated Rajputs and equated with Kshatriyas, while the bulk of the people who still followed their pastoral avocation remained as a subordinate caste under the title of Gujras. These Gujar herdsmen are found in greatest number in the north-west from the Indus to the Ganga, mainly settled or roaming about in the lower ranges and submontane tracts tending their herds of cattle.

Grierson suggests that the earliest known Indo-Aryan or Aryan inhabitants of the Himalaya tract, known as *Sapadalaksha*, were the Khashas, presently represented by the Khas clan of the Kanets. Later on the Khashas were conquered by the Gurjaras, who are now represented by the Rajputs, and also by the Rao clan of the Kanets which represents those Gurjaras who did not take to warlike pursuits but took up cultivation. Over the whole of *Sapadalaksha* the Gurjaras and Khashas amalgamated gradually and they now speak a language mainly Gujrari, but also bearing traces of the original Khasha population. Many of these Gurjaras of *Sapadalaksha* invaded Rajputana and there developed the Rajasthani tongue. Subsequently there was constant communication between Rajputana and *Sapadalaksha* and under the pressure of the Mughal domination, or much earlier in the time of the earliest Moslem inroads, there ultimately set in a considerable tide of emigration back from Rajputana into *Sapadalaksha*. The great swirl of population extended right round the Punjab. Grierson further suggests that during the period in which Rajput rule extended over the Punjab, the Gurjara fighting men were accompanied by their humbler pastoral brethren.

On the basis of archaeological evidence, Hermann Goetz[16] has concluded that despite periodical foreign invasions the eastern Punjab upto the Ravi, including Kangra and Kulu, the southern and eastern borderlands of Chamba belonged to the Kanauj (Thanesar) empire 'whether under Yasodharman, the Maukharis .... or Pratiharas', and that, 'in part of the mountains, at least, ... Gurjaras must have settled'. He further draws on linguistic affinity in support of it.

> For the Western Pahari dialect which now is spoken in Bhadrawah, Padar and Pangi on the Chandrabhaga (Chenab) in Chamba, Kulu, Mandi, Suket, most of Bilaspur and in the former Simla States, lower Bashahr, Sirmur and Jaunsar-Bawar in Kumaon (upto some miles west of Mussoorie) differs but slightly from Gujari, the language of the Gujars, the descendants of the ancient Gurjaras...... But as all such impositions of a new language in the course of history were the result of colonization or conquest (....), the introduction of a Gujari dialect like Western Pahari can be understood only as the result of a Gurjara conquest or occupation.

This event he attributes to the 6th or 7th century. On anthropological evidence, though 'less satisfactory' he identifies 'Bhadrawah, Churah, Pangi, Kulu and western Kumaon', etc., the areas where the colonization could have taken place. In the 'very characteristic type of costume' which predominates in the same area, he finds affinities with 'some of the Gujars.'

It has been suggested and believed by many, that Jats and Gujars, and perhaps Ahirs, also, are all of one ethnic stock because of close communion which exists between them. It may be that they are the same in their far distant origin. Their social standing being practically identical, there is no convincing answer as to why should they have separated into distinct clans. 'It is however possible that the Jats were the camel graziers and perhaps husbandmen, the Gujars the cowherds of the hills, and the Ahirs the cowherds of the plains.'[17] Grierson too has held that 'the

Jatts, Gujars, Ajars, etc.,' are related by blood to the Rajputs. Another interesting point about the Gujar race is their possible connection with the cult of Krishna. Rose's *Glossary of Tribes* gives the following account in that context:

> A problem of great interest in the history of Indian religions is the connection of the Gurjaras with the cult of the child Krishna of Mathura as contrasted with that of the ancient Krishna of Dwarka. This cult was, almost beyond question, introduced into India by nomads from the north, very probably by the Gurjaras. No doubt modern Gujars, even those who have retained their Hindu creeds, have lost all recollection of any special devotion to the cult of Krishna, and he is now prominent in the traditions of the Ahirs, but certain groups of the Ahirs appear to be of Gurjara origin. Among them we find the Nandbansi whose name reminds us of Nand Mihr, a legendary progenitor of the Gujaras, and a Solanki (Chaulakya) *got* appears among the Jadubansi. If we may assume that these two great races, the Gujar and Ahir, once pastoral, and still largely so, are really identical, the theory that the cult of the child Krishna was introduced into India by the Gujars in general or more particularly by the Nandbansi and Gualbansi branches of the Ahirs becomes greatly strengthened.

Conversion to Islam

It is impossible, without further investigation, to say exactly when the great mass of the Hindu Gujars were converted to Islam. Jammu and Kashmir Gujars and their Muslim brethren in Himachal Pradesh date their conversion from the time of Mughal king Aurangzeb, which is probably true though not conclusive. According to another unverified account, most of the Gujars converted to Islam under the influence of Khwaja Moinuddin Chisti, a renowned Muslim saint of Rajasthan. Fearing the wrath of the Hindus, they fled from the plains of Rajasthan and in course of time found refuge in Jammu and Kashmir, where the abounding pastures and lush green valleys enabled them to start a new life. Islam came to Kashmir in the fourteenth century. The possibility of Gujars embracing Islam along with other Hindus during that period cannot be ruled out. In any case when Babar invaded India in 1525, he found that in the Salt Range, the Gujars had been subdued and converted to Islam. (Bingley: 1899) That they retain some of the Hindu customs to this day than do the majority of their converted neighbours certainly speaks of the recency of the change of faith.

Migration of Gujars into Jammu and Kashmir and Himachal Pradesh

The period of diffusion and spread of Gujars in the State of Jammu and Kashmir is not known with any definiteness. According to one account they probably came to the hills after the loss of political power around the middle of the sixth century, when the combined forces of the Indian Princes under the leadership of Baladitya of Magadha defeated Mihiragula at Kahrur near Multan (520 A.D) and forced him to flee to Kashmir. Some attribute their arrival to the outbreak of serious drought and famine conditions in Rajasthan and Gujrat, their original homeland during the sixth and seventh centuries. Archaeological evidence shows that there did occur an extremely dry spell there during the above period, lending creditability to the theory of immigration of these pastoral people with their cattle to the green hilly tracts of Siwaliks and sub-Himalayas including Kashmir. Repeated foreign onslaughts and internal dissensions after 1000 A.D. had undermined the fabric of the Gurjara power and by and by they were reduced to nonentity by about 1300 A.D. During that period of disintegration, according to some historians, a significant event took place. It was division of the race into two main sects: those who continued ruling in small pockets were known as Rajputs and those who were driven out of their hearths and homes by the vicissitudes of fortune began wandering hither and thither in search of safer haven and reasonable living. Of these peripatetic Gujars wave after wave came to northern hilly areas including Kashmir where they found what they were in the look out, *viz.*, security and grazing and watering facilities for their cattle.

From Kashmir the Muslim Gujars first set foot in the then princely State of Chamba 'by the growing inadequacy of grazing resources'. That they came from Jammu and Kashmir is supported by a legend[18] common among the Chamba Gujars. One version, as given by them, is that once upon a time a Gujar woman saved the life of a close relative of the then ruling prince of Chamba, who in appreciation, permitted entry to the lady's relations into his domain alongwith the privilege of grazing their herds. The other account is that they were invited by a Rani about 200 years ago to ensure abundant and profuse supply of milk and milk products for the royal household. Rather than 'half-a-dozen generations' ago, as Negi puts it, Gujars seem to have entered Chamba more than two centuries ago. They had come there, maybe a couple of decades earlier than 1881, by which time, as per Census data, they had grown to a sizable number-906-is an approximation much nearer the truth. This assumption finds support in the *Chamba Gazetteer*, 1904. It notes that the Gujars came to the area only 'forty or fifty years' back and that they pastured their herds, by and large, in the Ravi valley and its mountain ranges.

'The traditional version of how the Muslim Gujars were drawn to Sirmur is rather romantic' says Negi T.S.[19] In his words:

> His Highness Raja Shamsher Prakash of Sirmur visited Punchh for matrimonial purposes. The profuse availability of excellent milk that he noticed at Punchh led him to the discovery of the Gujar tribe and their buffalo herds. ...... Apart from the matrimonial courtesies on the part of the Ruling family of Punchh towards that of Sirmur, the lush prospects of pasturage in Sirmur drew the Gujars strongly to the Maharaja's domains and some nineteen families migrated.

That the visit of Raja Shamsher Prakash (1842-98) to Punchh, if at all it did take place, was for matrimonial purposes does not bear historical scrutiny. The *Sirmur State Gazetteer* (1934) makes mention of his marriage to 'a daughter of the Raja of Keonthal, a lady of great beauty and ability'. It does not imply, even obliquely, that he had contracted another marriage much less in Punchh or Jammu royal family. But the fact that the Gujars is an immigrant tribe from Jammu is fully borne out from what is mentioned therein:

> The Jat, Sainis, Labanas, Banjaras, Bahtis and Gujars are all immigrant castes which have settled in and colonised the Kiarda Dun. Most of them are Sikhs. The Bahtis are an industrious community, and the Gujars, immigrants from Jammu, are stalwart and turbulent cowherds who winter in the Dun, and drive their buffaloes to the higher hills in the hot weather.

The colonisation of the Kiarda Dun 'hitherto a wild and densely forested tract' has been credited as one of the greatest achievements of Raja Shamsher Prakash. One would thus be on *terra firma* to conclude that a few Gujar families did migrate to Sirmur State from Jammu sometime during Shamsher Prakash's reign, probably around third-quarter of the nineteenth century. *The Sirmur District Gazetteer* brought out by the Himachal Pradesh Government in 1969, relates the event to eighteen-seventies. It would be fair to assume that over the next few decades a few more families followed the 'pilgrim fathers' in isolated and stray inflows.

In course of time this nucleus proliferated and spread over the adjoining forests of Simla Hill States to graze their herds. In any event they were noticed there by the turn of the nineteenth century. An inkling of it is had from the *Gazetteer of the Simla District*, 1904. In regard to forest management of the native States it reports:

The final instructions of Government were given in a letter No. 145 dated 15th March , 1888, to the Commissioner. Under these instructions the Chiefs were to be asked to demarcate the most important of their forest areas; to prepare a record of rights for each demarcated forest; to prohibit the breaking up of land for cultivation, and grazing by Gujars or other outsiders in the demarcated forests; .... Nearly all the Chiefs agreed to these proposals; and on these lines forest conservancy has proceeded in the States upto the present year (1903) with varying success... The rules regarding ...... grazing by Gujars have been more or less adhered to.

They had covered the territories of the pricely States of Bushahr, Khaneti and Keonthal, etc., is also corroborated from G.S. Hart's *First Settlement Report of Pabar and Giri Valleys, Pabar and Bushahr State Leased Forests (1906)*. Dealing with Gujar grazing it records:

In former years Gujars were in the habit of bringing a considerable number of buffaloes to graze in the Pabar and Giri valleys. This intrusion which was encouraged by the State officials for the sake of revenue .... produced .... which was objected to strongly by the people, gave rise to much correspondence and at one time it was decided to allow the practice to continue, but to limit the number of buffaloes to 500. However when final orders were passed on Mr. Moir's report in Punjab Government letter No. 189 S of the 8th June, 1887, the Lt. Governor expressed his opinion that Gujars and their buffaloes should be kept out. So far as residence within the State during the summer is concerned, these orders have been carried out, though in two cases they have been evaded to some extent. At the time of settlement of the boundary dispute with the Keonthal State two Gujars gave important evidence in favour of the Bashahr claim, in return for which the late Tikka Sahib promised them grazing for their cattle, and since that time these two men have fixed their summer quarters on the borders of the Khaneti State but have actually grazed their animals on the Chewa Dhar in Bashahr, while paying the customary grazing fee to Khaneti. Whatever service these men may have rendered to Bushahr has been repaid amply by many years of free grazing. At the same time the area over which they graze is bare grass land and they are useful to the State in giving help in the supply of milk, butter and ghi at the stages along the high level road from Bagi to Bahli. Consequently it is proposed to allow these two men to graze their animals on the bare slopes of the Chewa Dhar from the boundary of the Jubbal State on the south to the Ganarsi Dhar on the north. They will pay the usual grazing fee to Bashahr. It is to be understood that the permission to graze in the area mentioned is a privilege only, that it confers no right, that it can be withdrawn at any time and that it is limited to the following number:–

Nassar Din   ....   60 animals paying fee
Fakru   ....   70 animals paying fee.

The Forest Settlement Report of Jubbal State compiled in 1915 shows that besides 32 nomadic Gujar households who migrated for winter grazing or appeared in summer, there were 11 families who paid land revenue and had settled in the State. Between them they owned 279 buffaloes, 4 cows or bulls and 30 sheep and goats, as against 896 buffaloes, 110 cows/bulls, 214 sheep and goats and 3 ponies grazed by the outside Gujars. Grazing by both the categories, however, had not been acknowledged either as a right or the privilege and the State reserved to itself the absolute right to expel any one of them in the interest of proper forest growth.

They had penetrated into Mandi State and had settled there and were grazing their cattle in that territory earlier than 1904 is also a proven fact. It is manifest from the Mandi and Suket States Gazetteer, 1904. It describes Muslim Gujars (as distinct from Hindu Gujars) as 'exclusively a pastoral tribe' who 'scarcely cultivate at all' and 'keep herds of buffaloes and live on the sale of the milk, ghi and butter'. Though the Suket part of the Gazetteer is silent but there can be no disputing the fact that they must have gone over that State as well or at least secured grazing rights in its forests simultaneous to their penetration into the Mandi State. This is amply borne out from the subsequent Gazetteer of that State (Beotra: 1927), as also from the Forest Settlement Report (1923) approved by the Raja of Suket State on 14th August, 1926. It provides details of cattle of the four Gujar families 'who have been' grazing every year in Ramgarh and Chaosi Forests and of the fees recovered from them:

"	Buffaloes	Sheep & goats	*Dues realised
1. Lal Din	40	18 }	Rs. 105
2. Hasna	46	16 }	
3. Baja	17	-	Rs. 26
4. Taj	34	3	Rs 43

* The above dues are for six months (winter grazing). No. 1 besides the winter grazed his cattle in summer also last year (1922) on payment of Rs. 73/10/0 only.

The Hindu Gujars, almost all of whom, have since settled down and taken to farming are now found mostly in the districts of Mandi, Kangra, Sirmur, Solan and Bilaspur. They are either the descendants of the Gurjara tribe, who populated this tract during the Kanauj rule or those who later spilled over from the neighbouring areas of Punjab in search of better pasturage for their cattle and land for subsistence.

The Muslim Gujars, by and large nomadic, are presently concentrated in the districts of Chamba, Kangra, Kullu, Shimla and Sirmur. That some of them came from Chamba State too and grew roots in Kangra district in due course of time is amply manifest from Anderson's *Forest Settlement Report of the Kangra Valley* (Aug.' 1887), especially in the course of discussion about the grazing rights of both resident and nomadic Gujars.

33. Resident Gujars with *sawanas* are found almost exclusively in the Kangra Tahsil. Ban-Gujars have for many years come to Nurpur Tahsil and to Boh in Kangra Tahsil, which places are conveniently situated for Chamba from which they come. But during the last few years they have attempted to establish themselves in other places. The rights of the people in Nurpur and in Boh have been recorded, and Ban-Gujars may as heretofore come into these localities but they should be strictly excluded from all other places.

34. Sawanadar Gujars, whose rights have been recorded at the revenue settlement, and again admitted in the present record, may graze in their *sawanas* in the valley and in their *dhars* on the main range, subject to conditions recorded in the revenue settlement records and on payment of customary dues to the village communities. All Gujars, whether resident or nomadic, will be subject to the restrictions that apply to right-holders generally. They may not erect cattle shed on common land without permission, nor may they lop trees for fodder except within the limits fixed in the rules. The exclusive right of Gujars in their *sawanas* extends only to grazing grass and fodder leaves.

Notes and References

1. Smith, V.A., *Early History of India*, London, 1908.
2. Cunningham, Alexander, *The Ancient Geography of India*, Reprint, Varanasi, 1963.
3. Risley, *Encyclopaedia of Religion & Ethics*, Vol. V, New York, 1951.
4. Crook, W., *Natives of North India*, London, 1907.
5. Smith, V., *Early History of India*, London, 1908.
6. Russel, R.V., *The Tribes and Castes of the Central Provinces of India*, Vol. III, Reprint, 1975.
7. Ibbetson, D. & Maclagan Rose, H.A. (Comp), *A Glossary of the Tribes and Castes of the Punjab and NWFP*, Lahore, 1914-19.

8. Saraf, Suraj, 'Gujjar-Nomadic life, Rich Heritage' *The Sunday Tribune, January 11, 1976.* (See also 9 infra).

9. Hussain Majid, (Comp) *Geography of Jammu and Kashmir,* New Delhi, 1985.

10. Shashi, S.S. (ed.), *Encyclopaedia of Indian Tribes—Himachal Pradesh and Northern Highlands,* New Delhi, 1995.

11. Also endorsed by Goetz Hermann (*Studies in the History and Art of Kashmir and the Indian Himalaya*; Germany, 1969.) In his words (appearing as a footnote on p. 24) Indian nationalist historians have denied the foreign origin of the invaders because they later claimed orthodox Hindu descent. However, this claim is worth no more than the Roman pedigrees of certain early Teutonic conquerors or the Chinese clan names of certain Tatar dynasties. The early Gurjaras had names of Scythian character as proved by Sankalia, and the present Gujars, Jats. etc., have many Iranian or Central Asian customs. Likewise the folk art of medieval and modern North-western India reveals quite a number of non-Indian features. On the other hand, most of the Rajputs have been either indigenous in the area between the Indus and the Aravallis, or are Indian immigrants from Eastern Afghanistan and originally strongly infected by heterodox local or Sasanian culture.

12. Nesfield, John, C. *Brief View of the Caste System of the North-western Provinces & Oudh,* Reprint Delhi, 1969.

13. Munshi, K.M. *Glory That was Gurjaradesa (A.D. 550-1300),* Bombay, 1955.

14. Munshi, K.M., *Glory That was Gurjaradesa (A.D. 550-1300),* op. cit.

15. Munshi, K.M., *Glory That was Gurjaradesa (A.D. 550-1300),* op. cit.

16. Goetz Hermann, *The Early Wooden Temples of Chamba,* Leiden, 1955.

17. Denzil, Charles, J. Ibbetson, *Punjab Census Report, Vol. I,* Lahore, 1881. (Also see Bingley, A.H.—*History, Caste & Culture of Jats and Gujars,* 1899, reprint 2nd Ed. Delhi. 1978).

18. Govt. of India *Census of India,* 1961 - *A Village Survey-Maingal (Chamba) Himachal Pradesh; Vol. XX, Part VI No. 27,* New Delhi, 1964.

19. Negi, T.S., *Schedule Tribes of Himachal Pradesh - A Profile -* Meerut, 1976.

3

Gujars—Demographic Silhouette

Mankind is proceeding towards greater and greater homogeneity-racial, cultural and linguistic. This onward march encompasses a variety of dimensions and some agonising implications. Old cultures are either dying or are in the process of being wiped out. In this broad category falls a large segment of humanity known by a bewildering variety of names, such as, 'primitive', 'tribal', 'indigenous', 'aboriginal', 'natives', '*adam-jati*' and so on. Some major characteristics of these groups of people are their simple economy, unsophisticated rituals and social customs, small local community organisation and homogeneity.

Coming into contact with the 'civilized' neighbours, the 'primitives' of yesteryear are by and by losing their old character. Industrial civilization is now completing the destruction of their technologically simple tribal culture. Many authorities consider this process of cleansing or drastic modification of their culture a necessary concomitant to progress. Bodley, one of them, however, has observed that 'it is becoming increasingly apparent that civilization's progress is destroying the environment as well as other peoples' and their cultures. (John H. Bodley, 1982). The wisdom of endorsing and encouraging the disappearance of the peoples, who neither like nor desire it, and instead find satisfaction in their old simple life-style in close harmony with the nature and the environment is, however, open to question. To brand their economic system as backward and wasteful; their customs and traditions crude; and the people ignorant and superstitious, thoughtfully viewed, seems to be a travesty of truth and the ground reality.

Sociology of Nomads

For thousand of years, the primitive tribes in India have wandered in the forests and hills in search of livelihood, without more than a casual contact with the population of the open plains and the centres of civilization. Derived from the Greek root 'nemo' meaning 'to pasture', the term nomad generally applies to 'a person who lives completely from his flock and does not domicile himself to plant'.[1] Nomadism, in essence, involves the repeated shifting of the habitat of a people in search for subsistence. It is a regular, seasonal or cyclical movement, which is not unrestricted nor undirected wandering but is focussed around temporary centres of operation, the stability of which is dependent upon the availability of food supply and the technology to exploit it. Nomadic movement is distinguishable from migration, which conversely is non-cyclic and involves a total change of habitat. Nomadism assumes different forms mostly depending on topography and climate. For instance, there are nomads who hunt and gather, others who tinker and trade. Besides, there are pastoral and agricultural nomads. *Ban* (forest) Gujars in Himachal Pradesh and Jammu and Kashmir are primarily a pastoral tribe. Like all other pastoral nomads, they periodically return to particular areas, which phenomenon is more systematic than among hunting nomads. Such territories as they regularly exploit, they claim as their property. Almost the entire population of Hindu Gujars, who now live in permanent houses and own fields, once used to exploit the pastures of the territory they now inhabit though presently they combine agricultural activity with their past primary occupation of herding buffaloes in the adjoining wastes. The Mohammadan Gujars or the *Ban*-Gujars, on the other hand, possess neither a permanent home nor cultivate land. It is exclusively from their wandering herds of buffaloes that they continue to derive their livelihood. Their claim of inheritance or *warisi* in grazing rights of certain pastures and forests, which is as strong as that of land-holders over their fields, is nothing but a refined form of this trait.

Pastoral nomads retain their herds as wealth, while they live on milk or some of the young animals or on food derived through exchange. The hill Gujars' 'wealth consists of buffaloes, as that of the Gaddis consists chiefly of sheep and goats.'[2] When large groups of nomad herdsmen seeking land for grazing purposes come into contact with the agricultural land-holders, generally peaceful relations are maintained unless the later feel threatened of their grazing resources. Interestingly there is no contradiction over a Gujar and a Gaddi *waris* possessing a concurrent claim over the same tract of forests.[3] Since their livestock thrive on different kinds of vegetation there is little scope for conflict. Only when another Gaddi or Gujar brings in his animals or their herds intrude upon farm-owners' pastures there could be ground for resentment. Normally the pastoralist Gujars and the agriculturists co-exist peacefully inter-acting with each other in a spirit of co-operation and bartering surpluses.

The economic power acquired by families of nomadic herdsmen has very often led them to adopt a more or less sedentary existence. They have in such cases become attached to and even dependent on the agriculturists, with whom initially they had no exogamous relationship. When later inter-marriages became frequent, ethnical stratification turned into social stratification. This is precisely how the Hindu Gujars have assimilated into the local agricultural community and are now hard to recognise apart from them.

'At the present day' described Sir Alexander Cunnigham in his monumental work *Ancient Geography of India,*

> the Gujars are found in great numbers in every part of the North-West of India, from the Indus to the Ganges, and from the Hazara mountains to the Peninsula of Gujarat. They are specially numerous along the banks of the Upper Jamna, near Jagadhri and Buriya, and in the Saharanpur district, which during the last century was actually called Gujarat. To the east they occupy the petty State of Samptar in Bundelkhand, and one of the northern districts of Gwalior, which is still called Gujargar. They are found only in small bodies and much scattered throughout Eastern Rajputana and Gwalior; but they are more numerous in the

Western States, and especially towards Gujarat, where they form a large part of the population.

In the Punjab they essentially belonged to the lower ranges and sub-montane tracts; in the Jamuna valley they were almost confined to the riverain low-lands. Early in the nineteenth century they were found in great number throughout the hill country of Jammu. Here they were a purely pastoral and almost nomad race, taking their herds up into the higher ranges in summer and descending with them into the valleys during the cold weather.

Population

1931 Census shows that there were 15.44 lakh Gujars in the whole of the undivided India. Of them 1.70 lakhs were in Central India; 7.99 lakhs (283,495 Mohammadan males) in undivided Punjab; 0.90 lakhs in Uttar Pradesh and 4.84 lakhs in Rajasthan. In that year it was estimated that Simla hill States put together accounted for 82,000 Gujars.[4] In 1941 and 1951 Census Gujars were not separately recorded. In 1956, Gujars residing in Himachal Pradesh were notified one of the Scheduled tribes of the State. Incidentally the Gujars in Punjab are not so notified with the result that the population of this race hailing from the districts and areas transferred to Himachal Pradesh as a sequel to Punjab re-organisation in 1966 is not counted as Gujars in the 1971, 1981 and 1991 Census Reports. In Table 3.1, therefore, while the figures for the 1911, 1921 and 1931 relate to the total population of Gujars, those for the years 1961, 1971 and 1981 relate only to those Gujars, who belong to the Scheduled tribe category.

Table 3.1: Gujar Population from 1911 to 1981 Census

Distt.	1911	1921	1931	1961	1971	1981
Bilaspur	3333	3441	3193	4092	4911	6457
Chamba	1433	2673	2617	4836	6504	7519
Kangra	9595	9595	10375	-	-	17
Kinnaur	-	-	-	-	2	8
Kullu	-	-	-	-	-	1
Lahul-Spiti	-	-	-	-	-	4

(Contd...)

Distt.	1911	1921	1931	1961	1971	1981
Mandi	2375	2314	2963	3524	4560	6734
Shimla						
(Mahasu)	10112	9368	10563	1800	2151	1116
Sirmur	2639	2562	2540	2635	2506	4764
Solan	-	-	-	-	-	1501
Aggregate	***29640**	***30284**	***32403**	***16887**	***20634**	**28121**

(The aggregate figures are correct while the data of districts is not).

The unexceptional variation in population figures defies a rational explanation: the inevitable conclusion is that the data is far from authentic. As earlier pointed out, the 1961 to 1981 Census figures relate only to Scheduled tribe Gujars and exclude all other Gujars who are not treated as such on territorial consideration. Much reliance on this data cannot be placed for the additional reason that normally nomadic Gujars are not found within the territory of the State as they are mostly down in the plains of the Punjab and Uttar Pradesh or in travel status with their herds, when count is taken some times in September or finally in February. In such a situation omissions from the count are quite probable. Of all the reasons, it might be the strongest for the under-recording of Gujar population. More-over, the Gujars who are permanently settled and assimilated in the local agricultural community might omit to claim Gujar tribal status. This possibility cannot be ruled out completely.[5]

In 1980 it was un-officially estimated[6] that there were around 7,500 families of Gujars in the State. This estimate could not be fully cross-checked with reference to permit-holding families. However families identified in 1982 throughout the State comprised of 17,958 persons; average family size 9.1 persons. The average size of a permit-holding family no doubt is not representative of the true state because of frequent sub-divisions in joint families. It may, therefore, be assumed safely that the average size of a nomadic family would be more nearer to a contemporary settled Gujar family. According to a Government Study published in 1994,[7] amongst permanently settled Gujars, a large number, to be precise, 62 per cent constituted nuclear families with the size of a family, nuclear and joint, averaging 6.45 persons. It is happily in accord with the conclusion of another independent study, which placed family size at 6.67[8] persons. Of 7,500 families, therefore, the population of Gujars in 1980 would have been around 50,000 persons. The Encyclopaedia of Indian Tribes[9] places their population at about 46,690 of which 'approximately half, 22,678 are in Chamba, about 8,671 in Mandi and Bilaspur area, 6,670 in Sirmur and Mahasu, 5,336 in Kangra and Dharamsala and about 3,385 in Kullu area'. Of these, it is added, 'about half, i.e., 23,345 are settled and about 5,336 semi-settled in character.' Of 18,000 or so migratory Gujars about 14,000 belonged to Chamba alone. In order to settle all nomadic Gujar families, the Himachal Pradesh Welfare Department recently (December, 1997) carried out a head count and identified 1,010 such families. On this some what firm base it may safely be assumed that presently there may not be more than six to seven thousand nomadic Gujars spread out in the districts of :

Chamba	736 families roughly comprising of		4500 persons
Kangra	39 families	-do-	250/300 persons
Kullu	69 families	-do-	400/450 persons
Mandi	1 family	-do-	10 persons
Shimla	74 families	-do-	500 persons
Sirmur	91 families	-do-	600 persons
Total	1010 families	-do-	6260/6360 persons

Gujars as Scheduled Tribe

Gujars, a great historical caste, which fills some golden pages of the Indian medieval history, constitutes a significant segment of the Scheduled tribes of Himachal Pradesh.[10] Over all, it accounted for 13.8 per cent of the total tribal population of the State in 1961 Census; the percentage rose slightly to 14.5 in subsequent population Census of 1971; levelled at 14.25 per cent in 1981 and then jumped to 15.12% in 1991.

Table 3.2: Gujars as Scheduled Tribes

	1961			1971		
	All Tribes	Gujars	%age	All Tribes	Gujars	%age
Himachal Pradesh	122326	16887	13.80	141610	20634	14.57
Chamba	67058	4834	7.2	71464	6504	9.1
Mandi	5044	3524	70.0	5743	4560	79.4
Sirmur	2830	2635	93.11	3155	2506	79.4
Bilaspur	4213	4092	97.0	5236	491	93.8
Shimla/ Mahasu	3382	1802	53.0	3971	2151	54.2

	1981		
	All Tribes	Gujars	%age
Himachal Pradesh	197263	28121	14.25
Bilaspur	6604	6457	97.75
Chamba	95726	7519	7.85
Kangra	752	17	2.26
Kinnaur	44583	8	0.018
Kullu	7400	1	-
Lahul-Spiti	23766	4	-
Mandi	8022	6734	83.94
Shimla	3672	1116	30.40
Sirmur	4943	4764	96.38
Solan	1719	1501	87.31

	1991		
	All Tribes	Gujars	%age
Himachal Pradesh	218349	33028	15.12
Bilaspur	7983	7667	96.04
Chamba	111509	10741	9.63
Kangra	1620	-	-
Kinnaur	39609	29	0.073
Kullu	10914	-	-

(Contd...)

1991

	All Tribes	Gujars	%age
Lahul-Spiti	24088	–	–
Mandi	9417	7291	77.42
Shimla	4369	–	–
Sirmur	6113	5674	92.82
Solan	2449	1626	66.40

In Gujar population, Chamba district tops the list, followed closely by Mandi, Bilaspur and Sirmur districts in that order. In the non-tribal districts, Solan accounts for around one and a half thousand settled or migratory, mostly of the former type, Gujars. Elsewhere they roam about in winter season only.

In passing a clarification may be made here. It would not have gone unnoticed that the Gujar population rose from 20,634(1971) to 28,121 souls in 1981 but in proportion to the total scheduled tribes population its percentage actually came down from 14.57 to 14.25. The reason is not far to seek. In 1966, the State of Punjab was re-organized and the region called Lahul-Spiti with its overwhelmingly tribal population came over to Himachal Pradesh. The over-all slight increase in Scheduled tribes' population in 1971 thus caused the drop in percentage of Gujar population in the context of the total Scheduled tribes' population.

Age Group

Per 1971 Census figures, 44.07% of Gujars were in the 0-14 age group; 39.58 in 15-44 group and the remaining 16.35% in the older groups of 45 and above. The ratio of girls in the total female population was somewhat less than that of boys of the same age group.

It is of interest to note that boys and girls of less than 20 years in age constitute more than half, to be exact, 53.00 per cent. It is also significant that male children out-number the female children: the later forming 92.93 per cent of the former. The sex ratio is again higher amongst younger

Age Group	Males	Females	Total	Percentage
0-14	4745	4349	9094	44.07
14-44	4168	3999	8167	39.58
45 & above	1714	1659	3373	16.35
	10627	10007	20634	

Same factor as depicted in the Special Tables for Scheduled Tribes (Series 7-Himachal Pradesh) 1981 Census appears as under:

Age Group	Males	Females	Total	Percentage
0-4	2096	2019	4115	14.60
5-9	2209	2048	4257	15.10
10-14	1938	1786	3724	13.20
15-19	1505	1347	2852	10.10
20-49	4873	4709	9582	35.10
50-59	862	674	1536	5.45
60 & above	1224	832	2056	7.30
Total	14707	13415	28122	

persons (20-49): the women form 96.60 per cent of the males. Another note-worthy point is that there were more senior men and women than those bracketted in the 50-59 age group. Of this one possible explanation could be that the life expectancy among them has, of late, declined.

In 1991 the profile that emerges shows:

Age Group	Persons	Male	Females	Percentage of the Total Population
0-4	4737	2422	2315	14.38
5-14	8717	4503	4214	36.45
14-34	10780	5461	5319	32.71
35-59	6212	3244	2968	18.85
60-69	1351	752	599	4.10
70-79	659	354	305	1.10
80 and above	497	266	231	1.51
	32953*	17002	15951	

(* excluding 75 persons who did not state their age).

This time too the children (0-14) forms a significant segment of the total population—40.80% to be precise. The boys (6,925) outnumber the girls (6,529) representing in sex ratio terms the past trend. In the age group 15-59 again the women continue to be far less than the men. The senior segment (60+) forms almost the same part as was reflected in the previous Census of 1981. Their percentage hovers at 7.60 notwithstanding the rise in total population by 4,813 persons.

Rural-Urban Base

In 1971, 99.80% of the total Gujar population was rural based and only 40 (0.20%) were found living in urban areas. In 1981 the position did not undergo any material change: 27,985 Gujars were enumerated in rural areas and 136 in towns. In other words 99.51% of Gujars live in rural areas especially in most backward pockets and only a very few, rather a negligible section of them, has a presence in urban areas. The 1991 Census does not show any deviation in the settlement pattern. This time again the ruralities (32,720) far out-number those residing in cities and towns (308): the latter forming only a minute fraction (0.94%). Manifestly migration from villages to the towns is conspicuous by its total absence. It is a point worthy of notice. It is because of these demographic, social and geographical factors that their over-all advancement is affected and hindered.

Religion-wise Distribution

Contrary to the general belief that Gujars are predominantly Muslim by faith, Hindus account for a higher percentage - 56.96 of the total Gujar population. Interestingly there are a few Christian, Sikh and Buddhist Gujars as well, which is yet another hard reality belying the myth. All of them again are not nomads, which constitutes a minor part of the whole. The picture which emerged from 1981 Census makes following revelation:-

		Males	Females	Total
Hindu	Rural	8268	7622	
	Urban	84	46	16020
Muslims	Rural	6343	5733	
	Urban	3	3	12082
Buddhists	Rural	-	2	
Christians	Rural	6	9	
Sikhs	Rural	2	-	19
Total	Rural	14619	13366	
	Urban	87	49	28121

The largest number of Muslim Gujars hail from Chamba district-7,409 persons (M-3,835 & F-3,574) against only 108 Hindu Gujars. The next to follow numerically is Sirmur district which has 2,097 Muslims (M-1,133 and F-964) against 2,667 Hindus. In Shimla district they over-whelm their Hindu counterpart: 1,087 against 29. Hindu Gujars, almost all of whom are permanently settled on land and depend mainly on agriculture for subsistence, pre-dominate in Bilaspur (M-3,312 and F-3,055), Mandi (2,718 and F-2,650), Sirmur (M-1,429 and F-1,238) and Solan (M-800 and F-672). This phenomenon too is worthy of note because if it further expands, it would definitely have a cascading affect on their social set-up, customs, beliefs and values. It is also likely to wield some influence over inter-tribal relationship.

Sex Ratio

Sex ratio presents an interesting study. Over-all female population of the State in 1981 was 973 per 1000 males. Amongst Gujars the ratio was relatively lower at 912 females for every 1,000 males. As then so in 1991 it remains on the higher side as compared to the ratio of all the tribal communities in the State: 937 against 868. It is further revealed that the community is fast narrowing the gap between its male and female population: as recently as in 1981 there were 912 females for every 1,000 males. The ratio, however, is lower seen in the context of the corresponding figure for the State as a whole: 976 (990 for rural and 831 for urban areas).

Marital Status

According to 1971 Census 49.21 per cent Gujars were un-married. In 1981 there were 8,194 males who had never married: in other words the percentage of unmarried males went up by more than 6.5 per cent during the 1971-1981 decade. In 1981, 16,876 females were married while there were only 15,679 males of the same marital status. It would be presumptuous to assume that all the extra 1,200 males had married more than once, especially when the figure of widowers (1,541) is set against that of widows (3,270). More females in the age group of 15-19 were married (1,525) than boys of the same age (374) leading to the inescapable conclusion that girls are generally married off at an earlier age. It, however, cannot be read as the rule; for majority of the married couples belonged to the 20-49 age group (M-10,674, F-13,060).

Education Level

According to 1971 Census, 88.55 per cent of the Gujars were illiterate and only 6.35 per cent were returned literate though all of them had not received formal education: only 4.4 per cent had read upto primary or junior basic standard. In all, there were 118 persons including one girl, who had passed either matriculation or Hr. Secondary or Pre-University examination. Among 11 fortunate persons who had graduated only one was a woman. Actual figures for 1971, 1981 and 1991 are exhibited here below:

Table 3.3: Education Level of Gujars

	1971				1981			
	Male	Female	Total	%age	Male	Female	Total	%age
Illiterate	8647	9624	18271	88.55	10624	12194	22818	81.15
Literate	1035	276	1311	6.35	1831	745	2576	9.16
Primary	818	105	923	4.47	1809	452	2261	8.04
Matric etc.	117	1	118	0.57	397	17	414	1.47
Graduate & above	10	1	11	0.06	46	6	52	0.18
Total	10627	10007	20634	100.00	14707	13414	28121	100.00

1991

	Males	Females	Total	%age	%age amongst women
Illiterate	10594	13126	23720	71.82	82.13
Literate	2209	1191	3400	10.30	7.45
Upto					
Pry stage	2237	1221	3458	10.47	7.64
Matric stage	1727	409	2136	0.46	2.56
B.A. level	201	26	227	0.70	0.16
Graduates & above	77	10	87	0.25	0.06
	17045	15983	33028	100.00	100.00

The bright side of the picture is that the veil of illiteracy among this backward Tribe is being pushed back though the pace is far from encouraging. The number of literates which earlier in 1971 accounted for only 11.45% rose to 18.85% and 28% of the total Gujars in 1981 and 1991 respectively. What, however, is most heart-wrenching is that literacy amongst the women continues to stagger almost at the bottom: per 1991 Census it is as low as 18% in the State where the overall female literacy rate made a quantum jump from 37.12% in 1981 to 52.13% in 1991. Possibly tradition is to be blamed besides other handicaps arising out of their nomadic way of life.

Occupational Classification

By occupation 33.94 per cent of Gujars were cultivators; 1.33 per cent agricultural labourers and 3.27 per cent were engaged in live-stock. In the subsequent Census of 1981, 9,751 persons or 34.68 per cent of the total population were returned as main workers. Of 7,900 classified cultivators, one-fifth (1,655) were women. And fewer still were engaged as agricultural labourers: 81 males and 44 females. It is evident that live-stock rearing is falling into dis-use: only 874 persons (3.1 per cent) were shown pursuing this activity. Obviously the above profile is more true of those Gujars who have since settled on land and have opted for agriculture as the main source of livelihood. With them animal husbandry is but a secondary occupation, carried on in order to meet their personal needs of milk and milk products with surplus disposed of to supplement family income.

Notes and References

1. Seligman Edwin R.A. (Chief Ed.) *Encyclopedia of Social Sciences*, New York, 1953; Vol. XI & XII.

2. Punjab Govt. *Gazetteer of the Kangra District*, Pt. I; 1883-84; Lahore.

3. Barnes George C., *Report on the Kangra Settlement*, 1850-52; Lahore, 1855.

4. Shashi, S.S., History and Legend of the Highlands in *Encyclopaedia of Indian Tribes: Himachal Pradesh and Northern Highlands*; New Delhi, 1995.

   Male population of Muslim Gujars in Punjab States had been put at 25,885 in the *Hand Book of Punjabi Musalmans* compiled for Indian Army by Lt. Col. J.M. Wikeley (cf. Revised edition 1935; New Delhi, 1936).

5. According to 'A *Study on Different Aspects of Minorities in Himachal Pradesh with special reference to Gujjars*'; Shimla, 1994.

   'On the identification front, 46 per cent of the respondents have desired to be identified as 'Himachali' followed by 42 per cent who are desirous to be identified as 'Indian' and the remaining 12 per cent who have showed their fancy towards their own religion, *i.e.*, 'Gujjar'.

   This Study, it may be pointed out, is confined to permanent residents only.

6. Shashi, S.S., History and Legend of the Highlands in *Encyclopaedia of Indian Tribes: Himachal Pradesh and Northern Highlands*; op., cit.

7. Himachal Pradesh Government Institute of Public Admnistration. *A Study of Different Aspects of Minorities in Himachal Pradesh with special reference to Gujjars;* op., cit.

8. Shashi, S.S., History and Legend of the Highlands in *Encyclopedia of Indian Tribes;* op. cit.

9. Shashi, S.S., History and Legend of the Highlands in *Encyclopedia of Indian Tribes*; op. cit.

10. The various data relating to the 1911, 1921, 1931, 1961, 1971 and 1981 Census cited herebefore has been reproduced from the relevant Census documents published under the authority of the Government of India. Special Table for Scheduled Tribes for Himachal Pradesh, 1991 Census, is yet to be published.

4

Socio-Cultural Mosaic

Personal Character

The Gujar is a fine stalwart fellow of 'precisely the same physical type as the Jat'[1] but 'far inferior in both personal character and repute'. Gujars have been turbulent throughout the history of Punjab; the 'boldest cattle thief in the country', notes[2] Crook W. Babur, the progenitor of Mughal dynasty in India, recorded[3] in his memoirs: 'Every time I entered Hindustan, the Jats and the Gujars regularly poured down in prodigious numbers from the hills and the wilds to carry off oxen and buffaloes'. They were responsible to 'inflict the chief hardships' on his army and guilty of the 'chief oppression in the country'. Dowson records that the Gujars of Pali and Pahal became exceedingly audacious when Sher Shah was fortifying Delhi and he had to expel them from the hills with 'not a vestige of their habitation' left intact. In 1857, they are reported to have seriously impeded the operation of the British Army near Delhi. 'Their character as expressed in the proverbial wisdom of the countryside', observes[4] Ibbetson, "is not high one: 'A desert is better than a Gujar: where-ever you see a Gujar, hit him'. Again: 'The dog and the cat two, the *Rangar* and the Gujar two; if it were not for these four, one might sleep with one's door open': so 'The dog and the monkey and the Gujar change their minds at every step; and 'when all other castes are dead make friends with a Gujar.'

By and large the Jamuna Gujars were considered 'mean, sneaky and cowardly'; also represented as never having had any love for fighting and none of the character of manly independence. But further west they were 'excellent

cultivators' belonging to a 'simple all-enduring race, thrifty
and industrious' and 'a quiet and well-behaved' set of people
happy to be left alone in peace with their cattle and fields.[5]
Nearer home in the Kangra district they had shed all the
semblance of notoriety. To Barnes[6], the Gujars of the hills
were 'quite unlike the castes of the same designation in the
plains' where 'they are known as an idle, worthless and
thieving race, rejoicing in waste and enemies to cultivation
and improvement.' Quite on the contrary, the Gujars of
Kangra, according to him, 'were a fine race, with peculiar
and handsome features...mild and inoffensive in
manner...not distinguished by the bad-pre-eminence' which
attached to their race in the plains and certainly never
known to thieve.

The Gujars, the 'nature's own children' and 'lords of
forests' are a simple, inoffensive and generous people. God
fearing they have an unsullied reputation as honest milk-
men. Their credulity is proverbial: their women usually keep
the account of butter, ghi made over to the middle-man by
tying knots on a string. Sir Walter Lawrence[7] was not wholly
unjustified to describe them 'stupid and slow as their friend
and companion, the buffalo'. Not long ago, a Gujar in the
interiors of Shimla district purchased a pony and paid for it
on the instant. In less than a week, be returned the pony
and was more than satisfied to receive his money back
notwithstanding that he had to part with one of his milch
buffaloes for going back on his word. Even these days a
Gujar does not find anything amiss to purchase milk at
more than double the price he sold it to the same *halwai*
that very morning.

Physique

The Muslim Gujars are a fine race of men with rather
expression-less faces and large prominent teeth. They are
tall[8] and gaunt; large and round-headed; of oblong facial
profile; with fore-head and chin narrow and a long and
narrow nose slightly curved. They have generally good health
and attractive features. The aged among them betray the
rough and tumble of life in their sun-tanned and puckered
physique. Their looks bear testimony to the storms they

have weathered. The youngsters have ruddy wheatish complexion and are a picture of robust health. The women too are tall, well-grown, soft and gentle in manner with a shy and modest demeanour, which is indeed captivating. More open and frank in manner than the males, they would not tolerate exploitation and often are known to act independently of social taboos. It be said in their favour that they hold the marital ties in high regard notwithstanding the suggestion[9] of Barnes to the contrary.

In anthropological context they show[10] a preponderance of gene B (26.28%) over gene A (16%) in the ABO system. In the Rh system, they exhibit a predominantly R1 haplotype (56%) with a relatively high prevalence of r (25%) like many sub-Himalayan tribal communities. They have a high frequency of gene M and HP[2] (81%) in the respective marker systems and exhibit a higher incidence (42.5%) of non-tasters of PTC and a low percentage (2.5%) of G-6PD deficients.

Dress

The Gujars like Gaddis are a simple, sturdy, hard-working and virtuous pastoral tribe. They are peace-loving, polite, social and hospitable. Their love for their buffaloes, their *dhars*, their *kothas*, and the jungle tracks they tread, come rain or wind, is matched by the care and devotion Gaddis bestow upon their sheep and goats. There is, however, distinctive difference between the two, not only in their facial features and the animals they tend but also in their dress, appearance and language. Unlike Gaddis, whose garments are made of homespun wool, the Gujars invariably wear clothes of simple cotton cloth; blue, red or black colour highly favoured. A Muslim Gujar wears a turban, angled rakishly, vaguely resembling the Rajput head-dress, though not tied in their manner and style. With his trimmed mustaches and short beard, *hena*-dyed by the middle-aged and the old, a Gujar sporting the turban (*safa*) looks like a noble of Mughal court of yore. Invariably the turban is made of muslin cloth; worn white or dyed, mostly former, 3.50 metres long. *Lar* (streamer) is its free end waving over the shoulder. Some let it dangle on the right or left side of the head. The children wear *gujari topi* akin to *kantop*; its peaked top in different colour. As upper garment he wears a loose shirt coming up to his knees. The *kameez* is invariably of blue or black cotton material, though some times but rarely, he may be seen in a white shirt. Usually with a round neck and arm cuffs, more often sporting double breast pockets, its collars, cuffs and the pockets studded with densely stitched buttons has a lot of embroidery work. The younger generation prefers *bangali* type *kurta* like the one worn by the Pathans while the traditional wear is *kalidar kurta*: over the shirt is worn a jacket or half coat, they call *baskat*. It is mostly made of black material: sleeveless, is decorated with beads, buttons and frills displayed on the side pockets, on the back and the sides. Valvet or *shaneel* is the favoured material. A long coat is worn only when the winter is at its severest. Their *tehmat* or *lungi,* an unstitched piece of cloth, mostly of gaudy colour and check-pattern is tied distinctively without the aid of a string or belt. In winter a Gujar can be seen wearing a simple cotton or woolen *ghutana;* a baggy trousers, loose at the thighs and knees but fitting tight at the calf and ankles, where it rests in numerous folds. Pathan *shalwar* is also worn by a few and so is the local type *pyjama.* But some time a *tamba,* a type of shalwar, of white cotton cloth, which, does not go down beyond the knees, is worn. A *chaddar* thrown round the shoulders makes up his wardrobe: *poti,* a shawl normally 9 metres long and usually in white shade, on special occasions, and *khaisi,* a coarse cotton sheet, check-designed roughly of half the size of *poti* as an ordinary wear. With a staff in hand, the Gujars mostly go barefoot, but when out-doors they wear heavily nailed local footwear even when trekking over stony precipitous mountain paths.

The lithe grace of the tall and handsome Gujar woman is enhanced by the typical dress she wears: a loose *kalidar,* predominantly black *kurta,* knee long, heavily embroidered with criss-cross stitches of coloured silken threads and adorned with frills on the cuffs, collars and the sides. Very often it is decorated with appliqué work. By way of adornment, it is, most of the time, laced with coloured lining round the neck in different designs, to replicate a necklace, with similar treatment meted out to its sleeves and the bottom edge. What they keep in the copious side-pocket is any body's guess. Over it the women wear the jacket materially no different from the one worn by men. Their trousers or *suthan* are usually stitched Jammu style; tight at ankles but loose between waist and knees. Red-striped black cloth called *sui* is the preferred material. They are very fond of braiding their hair: numerous small divergent braids formed on the forehead slide down convergently to mingle into a single braid at the back. *Joji*, their typical head-dress, bigger in size than the one worn by Pangwal women is a cap made of cotton or silk cloth, mostly black in colour, with waist-long hanging tail in numerous longitudinal pleats. To beautify it, lot of embroidery work is done by the women themselves. It is kept in place by pinning it to the plait behind the neck. *Jhumb* is the every-day head-dress. A coarse cotton sheet is wrapped in a peculiar scarf-like manner to form a protective cover against sun and rain. Both men and women get their clothes stitched from village tailors. Rather than wash and clean them, the Gujars would rather have a new set made for special occasions like marriage and festivals.

Jewellery

Like women all over the world, the Gujar women too are fond of ornaments. But the general poor condition of the *hoi polloi* restricts their number to a very few mostly worn in the ears, nose and arms. No ornaments are worn in the head or the feet; nor do the girls wear any before marriage. Economically the community is far from prosperous, hence their ornaments are mostly made of silver. Of gold one among dozens would have one or two pieces. Various ornaments for the ears are *baliyan*, large sized silver ear-rings with bunches of tiny metallic flowers producing sweet tinkling sound on agitation. *Jhumkey* is a silver ear-pendent and so is *dod*, hollow, with the beads rattling on slightest movement, worn in the upper part of the ear. The most common nose-ring is called *ladang* or *koka*. It does not weigh more than 4-5 grams and may be of gold. *Balu*, on the other hand, is a big silver ring studded with semi-precious but mostly imitation stones. *Laung* is golden nose-ring of 5-10 grams weight and *murki*, a silver pendent, hangs suspended from the central cartilage of the nose. For the neck is *dodmala*, a silver necklace made of thin cylindrical hollow beads, and *hamel*, a heavier necklace usually made of silver coins and red beads. *Mankey*, yet another type of necklace, made up of small silver and glass beads is worn tight round the neck. *Naliya* is a cylindrical hollow silver ornament worn in the neck by means of a coloured thread. *Tabeet*, a tiny amulet tied with red or black thick thread and worn around the neck is most popular among them. It is an encrusted silver piece, square in shape. Sometimes a solid silver *nam* with geometrical designs imprinted on it is worn along with coins' necklace. Silver chains attached to the neck of the shirt and those worn in the neck are too common. Glass or plastic bangles (*vangs*) are items of daily wear though a pair of silver *kangans* may weigh as much as 500 grams. One or two silver or gold rings are now common among the Gujar women.

Their men-folk too have special preference for certain ornaments though the practice is slowly going out of favour mostly on religious considerations. The men used to bore their upper front tooth to insert a gold pin. Other ornaments losing favour are *murkis* worn in the ears and *kangans* in the arms. Still they retain their love for *tabeet* in the neck, silver cuff-links (*mogla*) and silver shirt buttons.

Food and Beverages

The diet of the Gujars is simple but wholesome. Excepting on special occasions, the staple food is maize bread all through the year: occasionally they eat wheaten *chapatis*, as well. It is taken with whey (*lassi*), and *dal* or a vegetable like potatoes or of any other local variety grown during the rainy season like pumpkin, brinjal, gourd, *ghondoli*, *kan guchhi*, etc. Green leafy vegetables whether home-grown such as *sarson ka sag* or abounding in the wilds provide variety to the palate. They gather roots, tubers, fruits and vegetables growitg wild, which add to the quality of their food. Urd, *mah* and gram are the pulses commonly cooked every day. Green chillies or raw onion is their salad. They have no special dishes worthy of mention save for *kheer*, sweetened rice and *sevian*. Only on occasions of festivity they cook rice, which is relished with jaggery (*shakar*), pulses, mutton curry and whey-curry, etc. Contrary to general perception, the in-take of milk both by the young and the old is minimal; butter, ghi and cheese are liberally served though on special occasions only. *Lassi* and curd feature in their daily diet. They are mostly non-vegetarians: pork is taboo and so is the flesh of dead animals and *jhatka* meat. Fowls and meat of wild animals they would relish any day. Islam has borrowed a great deal from Judaism including the concept of *halal* (lawful) — *kosher* in Hebrew — and *haram* (unlawful) including the manner of slaying animals for eating them. It is on special occasions that mutton is cooked in the house. *Desi* ghi but mostly mustard oil and some times of wild apricots is used as the cooking medium.

Alcoholic beverages are taboo as per the tenets of their religion but a few of them are known to indulge in occasional drinking binges. Salted tea and *lassi* form part of their meals, which they have thrice; *nihari* in the morning, *dupaihri* around noon and *sham-ka-khana* before retiring for the night. The left-overs of the previous night is what forms the breakfast, while fresh bread is baked for the other two principal meals. Roam as they do in the forests, they have the freedom to pluck and eat wild fruits like berries, apricots, peaches, figs, etc.

Smoking

Smoking is very much in vogue and practically every one smokes from the earthen *hooka*. While on the move, they make do with cigarettes, *bidis* and *chilam*. As a rule the women do not indulge in this pastime: a few elderly ladies form the exception. Children, however, are free from this curse.

Fuel and Lighting

The women collect fire-wood from nearby their *deras* but cow-dung cakes continues to be their chief fuel. To light fire they use the safety matches bought in the bazar. Gujar dwellings, especially on the *dhars* and whilst on the move do not have any modern lighting arrangement. They, therefore, carry a kerosene lantern alongwith their pots and pans and other belongings. Hung near the kitchen it is lit when darkness descends and put off no sooner the family retires for the night: saving of oil is prime consideration.

Cooking Utensils

As they are ever on the move, the Gujars have too few utensils to cook in and eat from. These are generally made of brass or bell-metal; preference being for lighter aluminium pots and pans so that they are easy to carry. Being heavy and cumbersome they do not keep either *sil-batta or chaki.* Grinding of spices they do on rough stones picked up from near their house or camp. Some of the utensils common with them are *aaftaba,* a *lota* with a spout (ewer), brass pitcher to fetch water from nearby spring or stream, iron tongs, *degchi,* a copper or brass vessel to churn curd in, *madhani,* the churner, *gagar, kadchi, ladle, katora* and *katoris, lotas, parat,* brass or iron plates for kneading flour, *pateela* to cook pulses and vegetables, *tawa,* to bake bread on and *thalis* (plates) to eat from.

Sanitation and Personal Hygiene

Personal hygiene leaves much to be desired. The men usually take bath once a week; in winter the interval may be much longer. But as ordained by their religion, they have to pay attention to their personal ablution; for before praying they must purify their bodies so as to render their devotion more acceptable. Therefore, if *gusul* be not possible, a Gujar must perform the *wuzu, i.e.,* he must clean his mouth, nostrils and wash hands, arms, head and face strictly in the prescribed manner. The teeth are cleaned very morning with a twig (*datan or miswalk*) : the women use dentifrice (*manjan*) mostly made of charcoal or dried walnut bark. Both the men and women paint their eyes with *surma* or *kajal.* The habit of dyeing the beard is common: beard is the sign of manhood and hence highly respected. According to their traditions all the hair should be allowed to grow or the whole head should be shaved. It is for the sake of convenience and cleanliness that the Gujars comletely shave their heads and crop or close-shave the moustaches. They say, and it might not be wholly correct, that their women bathe every morning. Since there are no bath-rooms in their lodgings, the women seek privacy in the cover of darkness of early dawn. Bathing soap is not much in use. The women are known to wash their hair with cow's urine, which is used to wash their clothes as well. Wood ash and soap nut are the other two natural detergents commonly used by them. Frequent change of clothes is uncommon. They are washed maybe once in a month. The blankets are washed once in six months and the bedding only once a year. As water has to be fetched from afar, they wash their utensils using the same water time and again. That perhaps is also the reason why more than one family member would not mind eating food from the same *thali* or drinking water, *lassi* or milk from a common *katora*, without first rinsing and cleansing it. The stinking heaps of animal dung in close proximity of the *kothas,* a fairly common sight, adds further to the terrible pollution of the surroundings and , in addition, provides fertile breeding ground for flies and mosquitoes.

Dwelling Houses

Gujars are not only a religious minority but are so occupationally too. As nomadic or semi-nomadic pastorals they lead a life pattern which is a far cry from the normal settled life: their peculiar nomadic life is marked by seasonal migration. Environment, in addition, plays a dominant role in shaping their life style. The house structure of Gujars is thus closely linked to their migratory way of life. Five months or so they spend grazing their buffaloes on the alpine *dhars*. Rest of the year they are either in travel status or down in the valleys. Most of them do not have permanent abodes: only those who own small patches of land can afford this luxury. The *kacha* shelter that they put up for summer camping primarily aims at meeting the challenge of chilly and windy climate. Though fairly large-50x40 feet-*kotha* is not partitioned into separate quarters for men and the animals, maybe to derive advantage of the body heat of the later. Rectangular in shape, it does not have more than one door nor windows or ventilators, manifestly to keep out the cold and the windy chill. For their structure no back wall is raised; in all likelihood to save on labour: the slope of the hill provides it *in situ*. The other three walls are raised simultaneously with rough hewn stones and timber, material which is locally available. The house is sited generally near a water spring or stream but invariably in a sheltered position.

The construction of the house starts with the digging of foundation (*neeh*). Among the Gujars Sunday, Monday, Thursday and Friday are considered auspicious for this purpose. Unlike Hindus they do not consult their priest. The foundation is usually dug to a depth of 3-4 feet and then filled with cubical stones. The stone walls are raised about one foot above the ground level when the door frame is placed in position. *Gur* or *shakar* (jaggery) is distributed when they start excavating the foundation as also when the door-frame is put in place. About 2 to 3 feet thick walls are raised to a height of 8-9 feet which are built of randomly sized rubble and wooden beams. No mortar is applied. In addition four to six vertical wooden poles (*thambs*), about ten feet apart, are raised, chiefly to bear the heavy weight of the flat roof. A framework of wooden beams and rafters is placed in position atop the walls and the *thambs*. On it a thin layer of either thick *grass*, *twigs* or *bhojpatra* (birch bark), whichever material be readily available, is laid. And on it is spread evenly, a thick layer of mud, which is held *in situ* by the underlying membrane. The mud is then rammed down to harden it. The six to nine inches thick roof is then plastered with a thick paste of clay, animal dung and chopped pine needles or wheat straw mixed with water. The walls from outside and inside too are plastered with the same paste. The floor is *kucha* and so is frequently coated with a loose paste of dung and mud. The roof projects by about two feet on all sides, and on one side often by as much as 6 feet in order to provide small covered shelter for the working tools, implements and fodder. On one end of the house, a small space is provided for the kitchen hearth which is secluded by a low wall called *oat*. But more often the hearth is located in one corner of the *kotha*, which is also the living room and the sleeping quaters.

In the portion earmarked for human beings, a small depression is made in the floor in which fire is kept burning right from early morning till it is put out around 10-11 p.m. After day's long work, the males of the *dera* sit around it to smoke *hooka*, gossip, to discuss domestic issues or to make merry. The useful purpose smoke swirling within serves is to protect the inmates from swarms of mosquitoes and flies, a great source of nuisance and cause of disease. Sleeping place is the raised platform along one wall. When moving in, a feast is given to the *biradari* members by way of house warming party. Gujars call this ceremony *nayaz*.

The larger portion of the *kotha* is used to tether the buffaloes mostly the calves. The slight slant of the floor leads animal urine to a pit dug outside the house. Every morning buckets full of urine that collects during the night is thrown on the dung heap. The *kotha* is bounded by hedges made of twigs and bushes with a small space left vacant for fixing a rough wooden gate. There is another opening in the rear of the house which provides access to the fodder stock. It is closed not by a gate but with thorny bushes. Often they would erect a *myahara*, an improvised shelter, deep in the *dhar*,[11] where their stay has, of necessity to be of longer duration. In the *dhars* no two *kothas* are observed within a radius of 3-4 kilometres. A kinship group of families might some-time put up their houses adjacent to each other.

Nomadic Gujars, by and large, needless to repeat, are landless. That is why they are considered ineligible for the grant of subsidy or loan by the government agencies and financial institutions. Their temporary *kothas* in the alpine pastures, they have to build afresh every summer; for no sooner they move down, the local graziers, out of envy or rather jealousy either burn or dismantle to a state of irreparablity. It is said that in Uttar Pradesh the Forest department every year puts the Gujar *kothas* to auction no sooner these are vacated on migration. As a consequence a Gujar family, including the old, the sick and the children, has to live in the open for a month or so till the old *kotha* is either repaired or a new one is re-built.

In the plains their houses are generally owned by the *zamindars,* whose fields they manure during their sojourn. These houses are usually 30-45 feet long and 20-25 feet wide built in the pattern similar to the residences they raise in the *dhars.* Building material, however, does vary according what is available locally. As Gujars pay no rent, they are expected to bear the burden of annual repairs. Result of a study cited in the *Gujars Nomads of Northern highlands* showed that 57.42 per cent of the Gujar house-holds passed the winter in hut-type shelters and the summers in 82.24 per cent.

While in transit they make do with a couple of tarpuline or polythene sheets which they pitch tent-like. Sometime they seek shelter from rain and hail under some thickly leaved tree looking in vain for a dry patch to lie down. For the hearth they raise a lean-to; but most of the time they cook their meals in the hollow of some projecting rock or in a natural cave.

For constructing or repairing their houses they never engage paid labour. All the work is done by themselves, both males and females contributing their mite. Most often *biradari* members extend a helping hand.

Gujars like Gaddis keep watch dogs. The fierce animals are kept tied during the day and are let loose at night to keep the wild animals at bay. They are fed on maize bread and *lassi,* the same diet the Gujars themselves eat.

Beddings and Furniture

Generally the Gujars sleep on the floor. Upon a thick layer of straw, they spread a mattress, home-made from worn-out clothes and tattered blankets. Durries, home-spun woollen blankets and pillows are the other items of their bedding. Some of them possess a couple of roughly-made cots, which they leave behind with the local *zamindars* when they leave for the plains. By way of furniture they do not have much to boast of save for a couple of wooden seats and grass mats.

Dialect

While generally able to speak the language or the *lingua franca* of the country they occupy, Gujars have a distinct language of their own, called Gujuri varying but little from place to place, and closely connected with the Mewati dialect of Rajasthan. Of course their vocabulary is freely interlarded with words borrowed from Pushtu, Kashmiri and what not; but the grammar is practically identical with that of Mewati, and closely allied to that of Mewari. Linguistically Mewari, Dhundhari, and Pahari form one closely related dialect group, of which Gujari and Western Pahari are nearest to each other. Gujars wander free over the mountains and have little intercourse with the other inhabitants of the locality. They have hence retained the original language which they brought from their native land of Mewat. But even here one finds in the specimen (appendix II) 'sporadic waifs picked up on their journey-stray Hindustani and Panjabi forms retained like solitary flies in amber, within the body of Gujar speech.'[12] There is no separate script: hence no literature in Gojri language. They however, employ Perso-Arabic script in written communications. A dozen or so words and phrases heard in the mouths of Gujars, from near Sahu (Chamba district) gives a fleeting idea of how close their language is to Western Pahari:

Addava	...	cattle fodder;
Gaini	---	cow-shed;
Kat	---	locally made scissors;
Jhero	---	pasture;
Kalauns	---	milk cheese;
Karrhan	---	cheese made by draining whey;
Khamba	---	dwelling place;
Koth	---	that portion of the house in which buffaloes are tethered;

Sahu bado sundar ilaqa ho	Sahu is a very beautiful area.
Hun it phaslo khari hougo	This time there would be good crop.
Tam khay karen	You are eating.

Social Institutions

Family Structure

It is a general custom among Gujars to live together so long as the father is alive and to separate only on his death. Small wonder that one comes across four or five brothers with their families forming one single house-hold. Mostly vertically extended, nuclear families are not un-common. The trend, of late, has shown an upward swing in partitions. Now-a-days within 5-6 years of marriage a son generally would ask for it. The cause mostly is petty bickerings in the family. The family is matrilineal and patriarchal with father as its head. On him devolves the responsibility of earning livelihood for the family, to manage prudently the family herd and to bring up and marry off his daughters and sons. He represents the family in all social groups. He does not act autocratically, rather he consults his sons and the women of the family in all matters, serious and non-serious. In case of an incomplete family, the senior male member is treated its head and only when there is no adult male member, the mother or the eldest woman becomes one.

The normal pattern of relationship between father and sons is one of superordination and subordination. So long as a son does not set up a separate family, he is expected to work for the family. There pervails an environment of mutual love and respect; age, sex, paternal and filial affilation, all forming the foundation of inter-family relationship. The family usually has a clearly demarcated division of labour: work is divided according to sex and age. While men tend the herds, do the shopping, deal with the authorities and inter-act socially, the women perform house-hold chores which do not differ essentially from those of females of other classes, rather is of more arduous nature. They cook the food, gather wood or fuel, grass and leaves for the animals, draw water for their families, milch the buffaloes, prepare curd, churn butter and clarify it to make ghi. To keep the cattle shed clean and carry manure to dung heap also falls to their lot. While the Gujars graze the cattle and frequently lie out tending them in the woods for weeks together their women repair to the market every morning carrying on their head pots filled with milk, butter-milk and ghi. Of charming Gujris selling sweet curd, Amir Khusro has said in his inimitable Perso-Hindi style:

> *Gujri to ke dar husno latafat cho mahi,*
> *in dege dahi bar sare to chatre shahi,*
> *az har do labat shahd-o-shakr mi rezad,*
> *hargah ke gui ke dahi lehu dahi.*

Woman's Status

The impression one carries of Gujar women, when one visits them, is that they are labour machines, but if one spends a little time with them, some other images also emerge. The care Gujars bestow on their womenfolk is almost touching. Woman plays a significant role in the family. As a maiden she more often ensures a bride for her sibling; as a wife she is truly a partner of her husband; and as a mother she ensures proper development of her daughters and sons. She has a respectable place in social status almost equal to the man. The Mohammadan society and the Law, as does the Hindu community, consider her status inferior and subjects her to myriad social and economic disabilities and inequities. They are not allowed to join the society of the men as they are not admitted to an equality with them. Even when walking together, the women would always follow the men, although there may be no apparent reason of obstruction to their walking abreast. At meal time too the women are the last to partake of whatever is left.

It is true that female children are not usually so well cared for and nourished as boys, and that if a lad and his sister were ill, nearly all the attention of the family would focus on the former. But girls are by no means treated unkindly and neglected by the Gujar community. In their parents' affection the girls stand next to and at no great distance from the boys.

Freedom to divorce is not peculiar to Gujar women: almost all the hill women, excepting of course, ladies of higher castes, do have this option. What is remarkable, however, is the fact that they receive *'mehr'* from their husbands, which the Hindu women do not get. The evil of dowry for the bride, happily, is conspicuous by its near absence.

Kinship

Kinship structure of a Gujar family is no different from any other Musalaman family. Because of their closely knit family and community life, kinship plays a very important role in their life. A detailed study would reveal tremendous elaboration of the tie, which in most other communities is fast crumbling. It is this system of inter-personal relationship which binds together individuals to one another by complex ramifying and inter-locking ties. It indicates the relationship of an individual by affinity and besides works as a support for him to lean upon in times of joy and sorrow. The kin ties do count for something. There are myriad ways the *Ban* Gujars are oppressed and exploited and the pain and sufferings they are subject to. One is, however impressed by their strong family ties and the importance they place on kinship. It is this human adhesive which has kept the community ticking.

The more important kinship terms are:

Father---*Bap, aba*	Mother---*Ama*
Brother---*Bhaiyo*	Sister---*Bibi*
Father's younger brother *Chachu*	Father's elder brother---*Tayo*
Grand father---*Dado*	Grand Mother---*Dadi*
Mother's Mother—*Nani*	Wife---*Gujri, Gaidri*
Girl---*Kudi*	Boy---*Jagar*
Brother's wife---*Bhabho*	Mother's sister---*Mosi*
Mother's brother---*Mamo*	Mother's brother's wife --- *Mami.*
Father's sister---*Phuphi*	Mother's sister's husband --- *Mosa*
Mother's brother's son ---*Bhaiya*	Father's sister's son---*Bhaiya*

Wife's brother—*Sala*	Daughter's husband---*Jawain*
Wife's sister's husband ---*Dadu*	Wife's father---*Chacho*
Wife's mother---*Chachi*	

Avoidance is not reported in the community. Joking relationship exists between elder brother's wife and husband's younger brother; wife's elder as well as younger sister and wife's elder as also younger brother.

Gujars greet each other by one reciting, 'May Allah be good to you' and the other returning the salutation by saying 'May Allah's goodness be bestowed on you.' The Arabic-Persian-Urdu word *Salam* is derived from the Hebrew meaning the same: peace. The Hebrew *shalom alech* means peace be upon you. From it is derived the *salam valaikum* (peace be upon you) as well as the response *valaikum assalam*-and on you too be peace. Young ones would be the first to greet an elder, who invariably would bless them in addition. Women greet by hugging, which is called *gullay-milna*.

The Gujars have cordial relations with one and all, belonging either to their own tribe or any other people of the area they live and camp in. They however, have a very narrow social circle and do not have any definable relations with others though of Muslim community. Gujar is a community in which peace and tranquillity in a house-hold is the normal phenomenon. Disputes are very few in number, and none which cannot be sorted out amicably or with the intervention of the elders of the *biradari* panchayat. Approach to courts of law is the very last resort: they would often relent even when their personal interests are seriously threatened. Disputes, whenever they erupt are mainly over pasture or land boundaries and generally on account of women. Petty squabbles amongst the women and the children some times flare up and involve the elders.

Islam, in its orthodox form, does not permit the differentiation of its followers into castes. In theory, at least, all Muslamans are brethren and can eat together and though endogamy is the rule among certain tribes and castes, there is nothing to prevent inter-marriage with strangers. But among the Gujars, the laws of endogamy and exogamy still prevail. Among them, there are, however, no inter-dining restrictions: they accept water and food not only from other Musalamans but also from the Hindus. To them only that food is *haram*, which their faith declares unlawful.

Law of Inheritance

Succession is bound by the age-old patriarchal line of inheritance. Property goes first to the sons and their male offsprings, *i.e.,* if a son dies leaving a widow, she takes a life interest in the share which would have come to him. All sons share equally, though the eldest gets *jethbar*, which is slightly more than what the other brothers get. The debt in the name of deceased father is repaid equally by all the married sons including the eldest: the unmarried brothers do not have any liability. All sons, whether by original marriage or *karewa* are on an equal footing and no priority can be claimed by the sons of any particular wife. An illegitimate son cannot inherit. A son is deemed illegitimate if born less than seven months after the marriage is consummated even though begotten by the husband; also if born more than ten months after the death of the husband.

In the absence of sons, the widow takes a life interest in the deceased estate, but where sons succeed, she has a claim to suitable maintenance only. A widow on re-marriage loses her right to the estate as also to maintenance.

Daughters and their issues have no customary right to succeed; they are entitled to maintenance and to be betrothed and married. The estate of the deceased is shared equally by the widows and their individual part is further divided equally amongst the sons of each one. If a Gujar dies intestate, his estate devolves on the nearest collaterals, the nearer male descendants do not exclude more remote, but all share according to the position which they occupied in relation to the deceased.

Adoption

Adoption is uncommon among the Gujars although the Customary Law permits it. A son-less man or a man whose only son has changed his religion, is considered competent to adopt an heir. The adopted son counts as a real son even if children are born subsequent to his adoption. The boy to be adopted has to be a brother's son, or if there be none, then a cousin in the male line. No relation in an elder degree than the adopter can, however, be adopted.

Functional Grouping

The transhumant mode of life imposes upon the Gujars the necessity to cohere into functional groups. The smallest group is the *dera*, a kinship group, which generally but not necessarily, is an agglomeration of joint or nuclear families. *Dera* or group is an important and effective social organization among the nomadic Gujars. Every *dera* has its own *lambardar* selected from amongst the elders of the families, mostly through concensus. To him are referred all social and economic disputes and his advice in family matters is heard with great respect. Acting authoritatively and impartially he provides a moral force ensuring cohesion. In order to ensure efficient grazing and care of the animals a few *deras* usually join to form a composite herding unit. Among Kashmiri *bakerwals*, the *dera* forming many herding units move together and stick together in the course of migration. Similar grouping, however, has not been observed amongst the nomadic Gujars in Himachal Pradesh. Instead they prefer moving in *kafilas* or caravans. A *kafila* is built around a leader, who invariably is the most knowledgeable person about migration routes and the weather and far more experienced in the geography of the country they have to pass through during their seasonal migration. *Buzurg* meaning wise, the *kafila* headman, is most of the time an old man possessed of qualities of head and heart. Formation of *kafila* is a compulsion forced by circumstances: it ensures safety and security of the herds and unity of thought and action. A *kafila* may embrace any number of *deras*, from ten to some times as many as a hundred families. Its membership is not permanent; it changes from year to year but not after it has once formed: So long the unit subsists, all the *deras* must subject themselves to the judgement, control and authority of *mukkadam*, or *kafila* leader. His is a very pivotal role: though a despot he has a receptive ear to the suggestions of other members of the group. Probably that is why he is held in high esteem and his decisions accepted unreservedly. His office is neither hereditary nor elective: more often he is anointed through mutual consultation and is the eldest male member of the *kafila*. In a *kafila* all individual herds of cattle form one common unit, sharing fodder equally and contributing proportionately to meet expenses on common necessities of the group. It, however, seems peculiar that the milk yield is not like-wise shared commonly: income from it accrues exclusively to individual families.

Biradari

There could have been no coherent social life unless the social relationship which binds people together, were, to some degree, orderly and institutionalised. *Biradari*, is their most important social institution regulating the inter-relationship of the members of the families welded together through *gotra* kinship or for territorial consideration. The head of each constituent family becomes *suo motto* a member of the *biradari* panchayat. In authority it is more powerful than a statutory panchayat. Its head, the *lambardar* or *zaildar*, relates the tribe with outside world. He is the hyphen that joins the community and liaises between it and the authorities. While he controls the clan and looks after its needs, the *biradari* panchayat administers justice in civil and criminal disputes in matters which had defied settlement at the hands of the head of the family or the group leader or a select group of community elders. It generally deals with matters of adultery, divorce and disrespect to traditional norms and although it has no legal authority, yet it is a powerful tribunal whose decisions are seldom appealed against. It passes sentences of varying degrees of severity. Sometimes the offender is ordered to give a feast to his brotherhood; sometimes to pay a fine; and if refractory, he may be excluded from social intercourse. In grave cases he may incur the most terrible penalty of total ex-communication, which is a great coercive force, more feared than imprisonment in a government jail. Gujars seldom go to courts to seek justice. It is only in rare matters that they are forced to knock the door of statutory *panchayat* or the courts. It is mostly when they are involved in litigation with Forest department or like authorities or when the dispute is *qua* non-tribal persons. The chart of responses drawn below proves this point.

Responses in favour of	Number of respondents	
Traditional or *biradari panchayat*	255	(85.00)
Statutory *panchayat*	17	(5.67)
Judicial courts	19	(6.33)
No responses	9	(3.00)
Total	300	(100.00)

(Figures in *parentheses* indicate percentage)

Cultural Heritage

Culture is a way of life and India is a mosaic of living cultures with a rich and hallowed past. Culture of tribal societies like Gujars, though primitive, still forms an integral part of it. Though wholly eclipsed by the tenets of Islam, the Gujars still possess a cultural heritage of their own. Art and craft apparently flows in the veins of their women. They are highly adept in embroidery work and shining examples of it are the caps, jackets and the shirts, their men, their children and they themselves wear. The walls of their houses provide them the canvas to paint virile and vibrating floral and animal designs. They make beautiful bracelets of *resha*, a jute-like thread. *Khaleet* is yet another specimen of their workmanship. An ornament just like Gaddi's *chhatta*,[13] it is not its replication. Made of leather and embossed with coloured glass beads, it is virtually a piece of art worthy of a connoisseur's notice. Their distinctive craft shows not only imagination but exhibits deep concentration as well. In a sense their life being more isolated, it functions within its own social confine. It has some times been defined as a tradition carried over vertically, as against the folk traditions which tend to spread out in diffusion. This inwardness has imbued their crafts with striking characteristics. They show a power and strength, a finesse that can only come from a painstaking effort, a deep concern for turning out the best.

Music and Songs

Contrary to the general view, music and melody are an integral part of the cultural life of Gujars. In the plains of Punjab and Haryana, the herdsmen and their women folk are known to sing a variety of folk songs. *Dholak* is their principal musical instrument. In Himachal Pradesh and Kashmir, however, the Gujars mainly play the flute. Very little is known about the Gujars and their culture since they avoid mixing with others. However a look at some of their popular folk songs does provide a glimpse of their sentiments, their aspirations, the romances and the like facets of their life. Their songs are strong in emotion and impulsive. They are true to nature and graphically define man's emotional reactions to the nature. Limitations in finding expression for intense feeling through rhythmic vocabulary are ingeniously sought to be overcome through repetitions of the same idea or feeling, or by piling up synonyms and expletives. Even through heavy verbiage, halting phrases or misty images, there does emerge startling songs of loveliness, at times, resulting in sheer poetry. Here are a few specimen:

In the following verse, both the God and the cattle, their chief wealth, are eulogised:-

God is great,
but our herds are also great,
for they provide milk,
which fetches us food to survive.
But God is far greater than the herds,
as he is their Creator.

A mound of stones near a mule track is held sacred by the Gujars. A young Gujar exhorts a way-farer thus:

Add a stone to the heap,
add a pine-cone to another heap,
then the goddess will appear,
before you.

Love forms an important theme of their folk songs as is
illustrated by the following verse:

A lump of butter shall I give,
you at sunrise.
Accept my greetings, oh
morning star.
My eyebrows you like,
Your waist I like,
I shall never be untrue.
Even the stones know,
that I am a good man.

His beloved responds warmly and with equal ardour:

The smoke rises in the sky,
Lift up your chin,
Look into my eyes.
The dove sits inside her nest,
The world gave me no peace of mind,
Until I met you tonight.

The following lines contain reference to snow and the
flute which symbolises all that is vital to Gujar culture:

You are so sweet, my love,
Like the sound of the flute, my love,
You are so pure, my love,
Like the mountain snows, my love.

Similarly:

The flute salutes the drum,
The Jammu night is a night of
songs and dance,
Do not play the flute,
Like an unripe fruit am I,
Do not touch me with your hands.
The night is too cold and long,
Wrap me in your arms.

Marriage ceremonies is a veritable treasure house to
string songs about. Sample this one in Gujri and see the
'solitary flies in amber'.

Too ten mili bichoriya sajna way too te mil mainoo
Charkha katan te mal meri ringay

Mere watna da ra lama peenga
Dame dam tursa mel mainoo.

Dance

The Gujar women do not evince much interest in dancing: their faith frowns on it. They, however, do participate in dancing on special occasions like marriages and betrothal purely for amusement and only within the four walls of their houses.

Folk-lore

The Gujar community possesses a considerable treasure of folk-lore and folk tales, which the elderly people enjoy reciting both to amuse the incredulous children as also to pass on the heritage to the coming generations.

Fairs

They have no fairs of their own. It is, however, a matter of joy and pleasure for them to visit local fairs and heartily participate in them. For example the Chamba Gujars do not lag behind any other *Chambial* in joining the festivities connected with the famous Minjar fair.

Festivals

Like Sunni Muslims elsewhere, the Gujars, in Himachal Pradesh observe and celebrate the festivals, which their faith ordains. *Muharram*, New Year and Spring festivals, *Ramazan*, the *Id-ul-fitr*, the *Baqar-Id*, *Id-Mala-du-Nabi* and *Id-ul-Zuha* are the most solemnly observed. The descriptive note which follows, gives some idea about them.

Ramazan: Many are the blessings promised to those who fast during Ramazan, the ninth month of Islamic year. The prophet has said that only those who fast with be privileged at the last day to enter *Raiyan*, one of the eight doors of paradise. During the fast, eating, drinking and sexual congress are forbidden as well as chewing of betel leaves and smoking. Those who observe this fast breakfast (*sahar*) between the hours of 2 and 4 a.m and take food in the evening immediately after evening prayers. On the first day of *Shawwal,* the tenth month, comes the *Ramazan ki Id,* or Ramazan celebration, when every one who fasts, before going to *Idgah* makes the customary gifts of wheat or other grain, dates and fruits. It is incumbent on Sunnis, both men and women, to undertake the pilgrimage to Mecca, at least once during their lives, provided they have means to pay the expenses and maintain their families in their absence.

Muharram: The name *Muharram* means that which is 'forbidden' or 'taboo', and hence sacred. This festival is observed in the first month of the Musalman year. It begins on the evening when the new moon becomes visible or rather from the morning following. The *Muharram,* including the tomb visitation (*ziyarat*) is said to last till the 12th day of the month, but the festival really lasts ten days. Certain additional customs are observed on the day: bathing, wearing of apparel finer than ordinary, applying of antimony (*surma*) to the eyes, fasting, prayer, cooking of more food than ordinarily cooked, making friends with enemies and establishing friendship, associating with pious and learned divines and bestowing alms in charity. The month derives its importance from the festival in honor of the martyrs. There are various accounts of the history of martyrdom of Imam Hasan and Hussain but all agree that it was caused at the instigation of Yazid. During this festival the musalmans are enjoined to keep their houses and clothes clean, and their bodies pure and undefiled. To have congress with women, drink any intoxication liquor, or to marry is forbidden.

The Terah Tezi and Akhiri Chaharshamba Festivals

The Prophet had been attacked by illness for thirteen days before his death. Hence the first thirteen days of the month *Safar* are held to be unlucky. On the thirteenth, all bathe, take some pulse, wheat and sesame, mix them, put a small cup of oil in the tray in which the grain is laid; look three times on their faces reflected in the oil, and each time drop a few grains of the corn into it. They also put some eggs and small money in the tray and then give it to some *faqir.* On that day they eat rice and pulse, sheep's head and offal, and send some to relations and friends. Others mix gram and wheat with sugar, coconut kernel and poppy seed, and after reciting *fatiha* in the name of the Prophet, throw some on the roof, eat and distribute the rest.

The *Akhiri Chahar* is the last Wednesday of the month *Safar*. On this day the Prophet showed some relief from the disease which ended his life. On this day, therefore, every Musalman, early in the morning, writes or causes to be written the seven *salams* or greetings on a leaf. They then wash off the writing in water, which they drink in the hope that they would enjoy peace and happiness thereby.

New Year and Spring Festivals

Musalman year, *Rabi-ul-awwal* is commonly called, *Barah Wafat*, because on the twelfth day, the Prophet, Muhammad Mustafa, departed this life. On this day accordingly *fatiha* is observed and all perform it because its virtues surpass those of the *Muharram* and every other *fatiha*. It is one of the three days on which Sunnis mourn, the others being the *Muharram* and the *Shab-i-Qadr*, that mysterious night in the month of *Ramazan*, when the whole animal and vegetable world (*kaainat*) bows down in adoration to the Almighty. *Sandal* is observed on the eleventh and the *Urs*, or death-day rites, on the twelfth. On these days, processions, as on the night of the *Muharram* take place. On the *Urs* they sit up all night reading the Koran and other sacred books.

The Shab-I-Barat

The *Shab-i-barat* is so called because on this night it is supposed that the lives and fortunes of the mortals for the coming year are registered in Heaven. Properly speaking only two nights are celebrated by keeping vigil, the *Shab-i-barat* and the *Baqar Id*. On this day the Musalmans prepare in the name of their deceased relations, stew, curries, sweetmeats (*halwa*), some of which they put on plates, offer the *fatiha* over it, and send portions to friends.

The Id-ul-Fitr

This is a festival of rejoicing after the tension of *Ramazan*. This month is also known as the 'milk month' because

Musalmans prepare vermicelli (*siwaiyan*). It is also called *Ramazan-ki-Id* as it marks the close of the *Ramazan* festival. Before they go to the place of worship (*Idgah, namaz-gah*) the devout distribute alms (*sadqa, fitra*) among *faqirs* and the poor. After the *namaz,* friends embrace and strangers shake hands, wishing them good health and prosperity. After repeating the benediction (*durud*) they kiss hands (*dastbozi*) with the priest.

The Baqar Id

The *Baqar Id* is held on the day or evening of ninth day of the twelfth month. It is regarded as a substitute for the sacrifice celebrated by pilgrims in the valley of Mina near Mecca. Stew, sweetmeats and cakes are cooked on the eve (*arafa*) as is done at the *Shab-i-barat. Fatiha* is offered in the name of deceased relations and some keep the fast (*nahr*). On the morning of the tenth they go to *Idgah* repeating the Creed (*takbir*) as is done at the *Ramazan* and *Id-ul-fitr.* After prayers sacrifice is offered in commemoration of Abraham intending to sacrifice his son. The *Id-ul--zuha* or *Baqar-Id* and the *Id-ul-fitr* are the two great festivals of the Muslim year and the Gujars observe them most solemnly as they do the fasting during *Ramazan.*

Recreation and Sports

Grown-up Gujars are usually too much occupied to spare much time for games, and these are consequently seldom played except by the young children. Nevertheless their forms of amusement are varied.

They are not given to revelry or riotous merry making: Gujars recreate themselves in several innocent and healthy ways. On festive occasions they would recite poetry, which they call *bait-bazi*, which often goes on for hours together. They hold wrestling and weightlifting (lifting of *bugdar*) and *beni* (wrist) holding contests. They in particular, are very fond of wrestling and exhibit great strength in wielding enormous clubs. Indeed sports requiring strength, stamina and skill are dear to their heart. Wrestling accompanied with the beat of drum is a wonderful sight which captivates the young and the old men and women alike. The melodious tunes emerging from the *banjali* (flute) keeps not only the player totally engrossed but seems to turn the entire meadow and its surroundings highly romantic.

Notes and References

1. Charles, J. Ibbetson & Denzil, *Punjab Census Report*, 1881, Vol. 1.
2. Crook, W. *Natives of North India*; London, 1907.
3. Leyden John Dr. *Babar**
4. Charles J. Ibbetson & Dezil. *Punjab Census Report*, 1881, *op.cit.*
5. Charles J. Ibbetson & Dezil. *Punjab Census Report*, 1881, *op.cit.*
6. Barnes, G.C. *Settlement Report, Kangra District*, 1850; Lahore, 1855.
7. Lawrence, Walter, R. *Valley of Kashmir.*
8. In Himachal Pradesh only 10.40 per cent people are tall on an average (*i.e.,* above 170 cm) and the Muslim Gujars (174.2 cm) are among them. (Cf: *People of India, Vol. XXIV, Himachal Pradesh*, New Delhi, 1996.)
9. Barnes, G.C. *Settlement Report, Kangra District*, 1850, op. cit.
10. Singh, K.S. (Ed.); *People of India, Vol III, Scheduled Tribes*; New Delhi, 1994.
11. The name *dhar*, which is the general word for a high mountain range, in a narrower sense is applied to a pasture ground; each run is called a *dhar*, just as it would be called an Alp in Switzerland.
12. Grierson, G.A. *Linguistic Survey of India, Vol IX, Part IV*, (reprint) Delhi, 1967.
13. Verma V. *Gaddis of Dhauladhar — A Transhumant Tribe of the Himalayas*; New Delhi, 1996.

* [Dr. John Leyden began translation of memoirs of Babur, from the copy of original Turki. He however died in 1811 and his labours came to an end. William Erskine wished to complete Leyden's translation but before his letter reached Calcutta, Dr. Leyden's papers had been sent home. Erskine prepared his translation from the Persian text end then compared it with that of Leyden and Elphinstone's manuscript of Turki *memoirs*].

5

Religion, Beliefs and Customs

Religion and Practices

'Islam', 'resignation to the will of God' denotes the religion taught by Muhammad, the Prophet. In it is included the observance of five primary duties (*ibadat*): bearing witness that there is but one God; reciting daily prayers in HIS honour; giving the legal alms; observing the feast of Ramazan; making the pilgrimage to the holy places at least once in the life time of the worshipper.[1] Another definition of the chief articles of the faith are: belief in the Unity of God: in His angels; in His books; in His prophets; in His government of the world; in good and evil as coming from Him; in the day of Resurrection.

Musalmans are divided into two main sects, the Sunni and the Shia; the former term meaning; 'One of the Path, a traditionalist', the latter 'a follower' that is to say, of Ali, cousin-german of the Prophet and husband of his daughter, Fatima. Muslim Gujars in Himachal Pradesh, one and all, are of Sunni creed, the 'Charyari', 'those who follow the four' including the Abu Bakr, Umar and Usman, the three Khalifas, earlier than Ali, rejected by the Shias: 'There is no God but Allah: Muhammad is the Apostle of God' is their *Kalimatu-sh-shahadat*, or their creed.

Sunnis generally offer prayer in a mosque (*masjid*) usually under the guidance of an Imam, according to its prescribed forms. The prayers are: (*i*) *Fajr-ki-namaz* or morning prayer: said from 5 a.m. to sunrise; (*ii*) *Zuhr-ki-namaz* or mid-day prayer, between 1 and 3 p.m. (*iii*) *Asr-ki-namaz* or after-noon prayer, from 4 to 4.30 p.m. or till sunset; (*iv*) *maghrib-ki-*

namaz or sunset prayer at 6 p.m. or immediately after sunset. This is of special importance and the devout do not delay it beyond that time; *(v) Isha-ki-namaz* or prayer when night has closed, at bed-time between 8 p.m. and midnight. The names of the five prayers are derived from the Hebrew. Although the five daily prayers are obligatory (*farz*) but fervour in belief and practice is usually confined to the devout only: a common Gujar seldom attends all the five prayers. But the Friday prayers he must attend. Friday, Juma, 'the day of congregation' is the Sabbath to the Muslims. On this day they believe the clay of Father Adam was collected; that on this day will be the Resurrection, and that during the last three hours (*sa at*) all requests are granted. On this day the congregation assembles in the mosque with the *maulvi*, who first sounds the call to prayer (*azan*) and thereafter recites the sermon, which consists of praises, admonition and advice. As a mosque is not always nearby, for instance, while they are on the *dhars*, the Gujars hold the service in an open ground made plain and kept neat and clean for this purpose. When no *maulvi* is available an elderly, wizened man of the group generally leads the prayers.

In matters of faith, a Gujar, illiterate as he commonly is, confines himself to the belief that there is a God, a Prophet, a Resurrection, the Day of Judgment and heaven for the noble and Hell for the sinners. He knows there is the Koran, the book of the God, which he holds in great esteem and high reverence, but in the absence of knowledge of Arabic language and of qualified teachers who can expound its meaning to him, he is mostly ignorant of its contents. He believes that every thing happens by inevitable necessity, but how far this is connected in his mind with pre-destination on the part of the God, the creator, it is difficult to say.

Though he repeats it every day that there is no God but the *Allah*, he almost invariably prefers to worship some saint or tomb. The Saints or Pirs, in fact are invested by him with all or some of the attributes of the God. It is his belief that the Saints/Pirs, if they are properly propitiated, have the power to avert a calamity, cure disease, grant children to the childless, bless the efforts of the supplicant to bear fruit or even improve the circumstances of the dead. The underlying feeling seems to be that man is too sinful to approach God directly and therefore the intervention of some one more worthy must be sought.

Islam presents characteristics of a well-organized system outwardly though. There are great differences of dogma, ritual and social practices between different creeds and people of different localities. It has arisen partly from the isolation of many of its groups from the centers of Muslim belief and usage and partly because many of its adherents have carried with them into their new faith some of the principles and practices which grew up in their original environment. Thus Himachali Muslim Gujars, converts from Hinduism, exhibit a few of the beliefs, rituals and customs which they undoubtedly have inherited from their earlier faith and cultural mosaic.

One such belief amongst the nomadic Gujars is in the cult of *Nag devta*, one of the oldest, possibly, in part at least, of aboriginal origin. It has a strong hold over their minds and the *Nagini devi* of Nurpur (Kangra district) is universally venerated by the Gujars of Chamba and Kangra. To propitiate her, every family offers a *bandha*, usually of *Rs.* 1/25 every year, which collection is expended on the annual feast (*bhandara*). Whenever a buffalo or cow is bitten by snake, they promptly pray to the *devi*, offer a little money which they put in a *lota* full of water alongwith a few blades of *drubh* grass.

They also believe in spirits, whom they regard spiritual beings. Though they do not have shrines or visible symbol, to each, however, a special virtue and a particular habitat is assigned. Their faith in Khwaja Pir is reminiscent of it. In all likelihood Khwaja's ancient name is *Varuna*. In his honour the Gujars make offerings of milk and ghi in running streams respecting each of their milch cattle, and if any one is sold to a non-Gujar, he too would continue the practice lest any harm comes to the animal. Khwaja Khizr is a saint in whose beneficial prowess they exhibit great faith, almost to the same degree if not more, they show towards many other Saints and Pirs. They would make offerings, just as the Hindus do, and whenever their prayer is answered or wish is granted, they would lose no time in fulfilling the *manauti*. Like Hindus, they believe that the sun eclipse is the handiwork of some evil star or demon; to scare it they beat drums, plates or empty tins and fire crackers and muskets. They too give alms on this occasion.

Their belief in evil spirits is common. Ghosts, hobgobins and witches they believe, are malevolent and no good would come by offending them. The *kalma* or the creed, for them is the panacea against *rakshasas, churails, devils, dains, jinns* and they would recite it the same way some Hindus would rote the *Gayatri mantra* to seek deliverance. Many are the tales the Gujars of Sahu (Chamba) recount of encounters with *churails* and *rakshasas* some of the names they give to the witches, demons and the evil spirits. Nyaz Ali, a Gujar hunter, they would tell you, once succeeded to escape unhurt from a *churail* who had appeared as a beautiful maiden to enchant him simply by keeping mum throughout the night despite her best efforts to make him speak to her. They believe that one should never travel at night with raw meat lest it turns into a demon. They also tell that the witch-craft of an orgess lies in her comb and when deprived of its possession, she is at the command of one who hides it either in mustard seeds or a pot of ghi or in a *syiul*, a receptacle for clothes. They also name many families, who according to them are descendants of the union of *churails* and the men, who had mastered them.

Magic and Charms

Though officially condemned by Law: 'As Ye have put faith in Islam, believe not in magic', they are no different from other Muslim commoners. They believe in the invocation of spirits for varied purposes including to secure the accomplishment of wishes, temporal or spiritual. Various charms are used to cure diseases, to cause butter to increase in the churn, or milk in a woman or in buffalo or cow, to remove cattle diseases and to make a husband obey his wife. Almost every child born in a Gujar family is seen wearing amulets. But the most efficacious way considered to ward off distress is offering of prayers (*namaz*): different types for different occasions and purposes.

Superstitions

These people are superstitious by nature and believe in numerous omens and superstitions. For them certain days are lucky like Thursday or Friday to start a journey and Thursday, Friday and Sunday to solemnise marriage. Friday being the most auspicious, Gujars consider it sacrilegious to sell milk, curd, ghi or any other milk product that day. For shaving, the best days are Monday, Wednessday, Thursday and Friday, the other days of the week being considered inauspicious. Certain days are prescribed for bathing. If a person bathes on Sunday he will suffer affliction; on Monday, his goods will be increased; on Tuesday, he will suffer from anxiety of mind; on Wednesday, his property will increase; on Friday, all his sins will be forgiven; and on Saturday, all his ailments will be removed. Some of them are so superstitious that they would never transact any important business without first referring to the *maulvi* or the Koran for an augury.

Maulvi

Maulvi, their religious leader and preceptor, though not of their community, lives and moves with Gujar families, with whom he attaches himself. His principal duty is to cater to their faith and perform all religious ceremonies and rituals. In addition he is the teacher of their children, whom he imparts elementary knowledge of Urdu and some times of Arabic to make them capable of learning Koran: his main emphasis is focused on traditional religious education. As he has no other means of livelihood, he is totally dependent on the Gujars to feed and clothe him. By way of income he receives usual fees for officiating at ceremonies connected with birth, marriage, death and the like. He is also the recipient of the alms they give on occasions of various festivals. His services as an astrologer and writer of charms and amulets to ward off evil spirits is always in demand. Superstitious by nature, the Gujars must consult him whenever they have to take important decision, be it the concern of family or business. His position in the community is of great prestige and his stranglehold on their social, religious, educational and family life is total, if not absolute.

Mythology

'The myth is a narrative of events, the socially sanctioned narratives of these events, the traces which they left behind as part of their super-natural powers.'[2] A myth is the 'dream thinking' of the people just as the dream is the myth of an individual. Myths are those sacred tales with which men seek to invest their lives with cosmic grandeur. A myth frequently seeks to postulate a 'time before time, a kind of sacred pre-history, a drowsy surrealistic world in which the coordinates of time and space are suspended and shifting, and nothing is impossible' says I.M. Lewis, anthropologist. But myths donot end merely in the telling of a tale. On the contrary they have various sociological and psychological nuances and are, even considered as the 'soul stuff' of social anthropology. Verrier Elwin defined it aptly when he said the myths make every thing contemporary, for they give vitality to customs, institutions and obligations. In the institutional life of Gujars, myths have been observed to impress their social customs and practices. The Gujars of the Khatana clan believe that a child born out of wed-lock was left by his mother in a lonely jungle, where he was brought up by a peahen. A hunter, who one day killed the peahen took the child home and reared him as his own son. When Kasam, the name hunter gave him, grew up, he married a daughter of Raja Anand Pal. Khatanas claim descent from him, and as a tribute to the peahen, members of this clan hold the peacock in high esteem equal to what the cow is to Hindus. They even swear by peacock.

Another legend associated with the same clan is that one day Mor and Mohang, sons of Raja Bhans, came back from hunting and ate food while sitting on a *khat*. For this breach of social ettiquette the Brahmans outcasted them and they adopted Islam. Ever since they have been nick-named Khatanas from the term *khat*.[3]

Likewise the Gujars of Lodhe clan claim to be genealogical descendants of Raja Luddar Singh of Jammu. The story[4] is that their ancestress was a beautiful Gujri, who, while going along with a water-pot on her head, stopped a run-away buffalo by pressing her foot on the rope tied to its neck, and did so without spilling even a drop of water. This feat of strength so pleased Raja Luddar Singh, who was looking on, that he immediately placed her in his *zanana* and changed his religion and name to Luddar Hussain. Thus a new *got* or family sprang up. As the progeny of a king the Lodhas claim superiority over other Gujar clans.

The Kasana Gujars, who claim their descent from Raja Kans, the maternal uncle of lord Krishna, swear by lightening and do not keep any bronze utensil in their households.

This legend relates to the creation of the world. It is said that when God created earth, it was just a vast flat expanse of land, circular in shape like the bottom of a dish. Lest the oceans spill over, he placed mountains all around. As the mountains were nearer to the Sun, they used to get fiercely scorched. Responding to their entreaties to save them from the hellish fire, the God made them cooler than plains notwithstanding their proximity to the Sun.

Customs

It is generally asserted[5] that the real (*asli*) or original Gujars are the 2-1/2 sections namely, Kasana, Gursi and the half tribe of Burgat, so called as descended from a slave mother. Next to these rank the Khatanas, who for a long period held sway in Gujrat, in which tract, however, the 2-1/2 sections were the original settlers, the other sections having become affiliated to them in course of time, though not necessarily Gujar by origin.

The Gujurs are often said to have 84 clans and in Ludhiana their *mirasis* address them as '*chaurasi got da diwa*', i.e., 'light of 84 clans' but other accounts assign them 101, 170 or even 388 sections. Of the numerous clans none has any definite superiority over the rest. Some Gujars who donot allow their women to go into the towns with milk regard themselves as superior to those who allow this practice and refuse them daughters in marriage.

The Gujars are divided into two endogamous religious groups: the Muslims and the Hindus. The Muslims have two sections, *i.e.,* Bhatariye and Bhanariye, who normally donot inter-marry. They are further segmented into exogamous *gotras viz.,* Bhatti, Chandel, Chauhan, Banja, Lodha, Kasana, Bhensi, Chopra, Chechi, Khatana, Padha and many more, which no doubt, are their past Hindu clans.[6] Though believing in the reality of blood ties on the patrilineal lines, they neither have any localized clans nor possess any tendency towards local exogamy or endogamy. In this sense, they can be called agamous as per G.P. Murdock's definition *(The World Ethnographic Sample)*. The prohibition against clan endogamy, a special feature of clan custom, is missing these days mostly because of their Islamization. Among the Gujars of Himachal Pradesh marriage may be contracted among near relatives but the *gotra* is invariably taken into account, for their belief in *gotra* exogamy surpasses all religious injunctions.

Rites de Passage

The principal phases in the life of a Gujar are celebrated by a number of ceremonies and rituals. These commence from the time anterior to his birth, when the mother first indulges in the hope of an offspring and attend almost every important incident of his life until his soul is supposed to wing its flight to another world the most important relate to birth, marriage and death.

Birth-Customary Rites

Though the desire for male offspring does not influence the Gujars to the same extent as is the longing of Hindus, his neighbours, they still have an intense craving for a male heir. They therefore employ many devices to relieve barren-ness in their women as also to ensure birth of a son rather than a daughter. When conception is announced, the expectant mother is subjected to various taboos and she takes various precautions to avoid attack of evil spirits. She is barred from entering a shed used at marriage or other festivities; from viewing the face of a dead person or visiting haunted places such as graveyard. She is not given anything to eat during eclipse. During pregnancy she avoids wearing new clothes, or ornaments nor does she apply *kajal* to the eyes or *hena* to hands or feet. These things, the people believe, tempt the evil eye. Many of the taboos, it has been observed, have been borrowed from the Hindus.

It is a general custom that the first child should be born at the house of the mother's parents. A separate room or mostly a corner in the house is arranged, cleaned and made fit for the purpose. Fire is kept burning in order to defend the mother and the child from evil spirits. Many charms are used to aid delivery. In labour she is assisted by a mid-wife or old ladies of the community. Immediately after delivery she is given some herbal concoction to induce expulsion of placenta; which when cut with a pair of scissors or any other sharp instrument, is buried in the ground near the house. The drink commonly given to the mother for a fortnight or so is *Achwani*, so called because it is water boiled with ajwain (*Iigusticum ajowan*). She is given *sonthaura*, made of dry ginger (*sonth*) fried in ghi along with sugar and dry fruits. Her diet mostly consists of rice boiled in milk with plenty of ghi added. For about a fortnight or even more the family would insist on her drinking good amount of milk two to three times a day. This to ensure that the child is not in want of mother's milk: she breast feeds the child for two to three years. The woman is looked after by the mid-wife for ten to fifteen days depending on the mother's situation. It is only when she is stronger in body that she takes over the care of the child and the house-hold chores. It would really be a crisis situation for the mother, the new-born and the family were the delivery to take place while the *dera* is on the move: perforce the mother would not be allowed much rest.

Soon after birth the mid-wife gives the baby *ghutti*, a cleansing medicine. The glad tidings are communicated to relatives and friends and *gur* and *batashas* are distributed to express joy and happiness. On the birth of the first child and more so of a son, the girls of the *dera* join and sing appropriate congratulatory songs. The mid-wife is given a present normally of one rupee and a shirt-piece. After the child is washed and swaddled, he is presented to the relatives and friends. The *azan* is whispered thrice in his right ear and the *kalima* in the left. This is generally done by the *maulvi*, or by an elderly person.

The naming of the child is often done on the day of birth itself or on that day next week: generally the former is chosen. In almost all cases, the parents are agreed on the name in advance. It is their discretion or of the family elders; advice of *maulvi* is not essential. The impurity of the mother lasts for 40 days. During this period she is not allowed to pray, to touch Koran, enter a mosque or milk cows or buffaloes. These taboos originally lasted as long as any issue of blood continued. Cooking and other house-hold work, though, she takes up after the ritual bath on the seventh day.

Most of the Gujars combine birth sacrifice with the first shaving of the hair. The traditions allow *aqiqa* to be performed at any time in the life time of a man or even after his death by his son. One or two goats or sheep are sacrificed in the name of God: an offering 'in the stead of son, life for life, blood for blood, head for head, bone for bone, hair for hair and skin for skin.'[7] It has been noticed that as Islam does not permit person in debt to perform this ritual, animal sacrifice among Ban-Gujars is a rare sight: most of the Gujars are most of the time in debt. The Gujar feast given to all the relations and the *biradari* usually consists of rice, mutton and tea, in addition to a few other preparations. Hair for the first time is cut on an auspicious day normally after the child is six months' old either by the mother or the mid-wife. The ritualistic shaving accompanied by giving of alms may follow any time later.

No married Gujri would be seen without numerous ear and nose rings. By way of advance action, any time when a girl is of three to nine years old, a barber, or any woman or goldsmith would prick her ears and nose. Usually this is done with a sewing needle during the winter months when there is little risk of infection. Except for mustard oil no ointment or medicine is applied to hasten the healing process. Lest the holes heal completely thread rings are passed through the bores. By degrees many more holes are bored till she has 13 holes in the right and 12 in the left ear.

The rite of initiation, *Bi'smillah*, 'pronouncing the name of God', is observed when the son or the daughter has reached the age of four years, four months and four days. The first sentence of the Koran, considered to be of high value, is taught to the child. This is done by the child's tutor or the *maulvi*, to whom some presents are given.

Circumcision (*khatna, sunnat*), is performed upto the age of twelve or fourteen years though it is lawful to do it seven days after birth. Among Gujars, it is usually done soon after the boy is two years' old on an auspicious day forecast by the *maulvi*. The boy is seated on a new large earthen pot inverted or on a stool with a red handkerchief spread over it. Usually the boy is dosed with the electuary known as *majun*, an hour or so before the operation. Some friends hold the boy firmly and the barber performs the operation with a sharp razor. He applies a dressing of some ointment or warm ash of cow-dung and the wound heals in the course of a week or so. While the rite is going on, some rice and other gifts are laid close by, which are later given to the barber. Normally a boy would not be circumcised alone but always with another to make the number equal. They think it favourable if the boy during the operation makes water, as this clears the urethra. Care is taken of the severed foreskin lest a witch may work evil magic by means of it . After operation they guard the boy against contact with dogs or cats and from other defilements. After a week or so, when the wound has completely healed, the boy is given the ritual bath and given new clothes to wear. On this day all such relatives who have not already done so on the day of circumcision give the boy the customary present of some money, any amount between two to five rupees. In some families, a young girl from another family, applies *hena* to the boy and thus becomes her god-sister. With the reciting of Koran, the ceremony comes to an end. The feast given on this occasion mostly comprises of rice, milk and sugar. The barber is given some present, in cash or in kind.

Marriage

Marriage is enjoined on every Musalaman and celibacy was condemned by the Prophet. Himachali Muslim Gujars form no exception. What, however, sets them apart is that they consider marriage a sacrosanct union and not a contract as the Musalamans at large hold. Polyandry is abhorrent and polygamy a rare phenomenon although

Muslim personal law allows them as many as four wives at a time.[8] They provide another distinguishing feature in that they donot exhibit any special tendency towards clan endogamy, a special feature of clan custom. They also donot show any particular preference for the first or second cousin unions: Islam permits marriage between cousins of all shades and degree. The prohibited degrees of marriage are determined on grounds of consanguinity, affinity and fosterage. The proscriptions laid down by their religion is against marriage of persons more nearly related. The *gotra* exogamy is the additional test Himachali Gujars are seriously concerned about.

According to the Muslim Law, a boy should be married at puberty, a girl at the age of twelve. Among the Mohammadans of North India however the practice is to marry youths when eighteen and girls after fourteen years of age. Gujars more or less adhere to it: application of law of averages shows that they marry sons between the age of 16-18 and daughters when they are 15-17 years old. Isolated cases of early marriage are exception to the rule. Their morality is highly commendable; they are remarkably free from any pre-marital relationship.

Family planning in Gujar families is an unknown practice. Researchers say that although 82.67 per cent of the three hundred Gujars they contacted, were fully aware of the government family planning programme, not a single one admitted practicing any recommended method. They are reluctant to own it for the simple reason that it has no religious sanction. In fact their religious preceptors frown upon it and often declare it unislamic in concept. Moreover every family needs more working hands. They, however, do follow the traditional taboos or proscriptions laid for the couples.

Forms of Marriage

By dower: Marriage is usually by dower or settlement (*mahr*) which is 'not the exchange or consideration given by the man to the woman for entering into the contract, but imposed by law on the husband as a token of respect for its subject, the woman'. It is the most respectable form of marriage, arranged with the consent of the parties.

By purchase: Marriage by purchase, however, is more common among the Gujars. The father of the bridegroom pays the price to the father of the bride. It may range between 2,500 to 10,000 rupees. The *biradari* disapproves it and has taken steps to eliminate what they consider an evil practice: the crusade seems to be gaining acceptability as, of late, there has been substantial decline in the amount of bride price. Indebtedness of the family and lack of harmony between the partners are its two obvious ill-effects.

By exchange: Popularly called *sata-bata* (barter), a boy gets a wife in exchange for a girl married to the brother of the wife. Real or a cousin sister is usually given in exchange. Unilateral marriages is the general rule; multi-lateral connexions too are fairly common. For example if boy A is married to B's sister, B in exchange, receives in wedlock a sister of A: again, A marries a sister of B, who marries a sister of C, who, in turn, becomes the husband of a sister of A. This system is widely prevalent and, in totality, it accounts for more marriages than by all other methods combined. Sadly it often results in wide age difference between the two. Moreover because of its dominant prevalence many a poor young men remain un-married because of inability to offer a sister in exchange or raise the bride money.

By service: It is a typical type of marriage in vogue in the community. In order to earn the hand of a girl, a boy, oft-times of a poorer family, serves the prospective in-laws for a number of years—5 to 10 years—though the common term is 7 years. During this period the would-be-bridegroom stays with the in-laws and works whole-time as an unpaid domestic worker. But if he works seasonally or on part-time basis, the period of service is extended. After marriage, however, he is not bound to serve the in-laws or stay at their place.

Ghar-Jawantru: This is an interesting marriage institution in vogue amongst the Gujars. With the passage of time its incidence is on the decline. Mostly a family which has a large number of daughters but no son invites the boy to work and live in the house. He is adopted by the parents of the girl and inherits the estate on the death of his father-in-law. There have also been cases when a father rich enough to part with a part of his herd, has found a life partner for one of his daughters without formally adopting him.

By elopement: Elopement, which is generally frowned upon by the community and casts social stigma on the woman, is a feature not unknown to the tribe. It eventually ends in marriage, of course, with the consent of the couple and approval of the *biradari*, which is accorded only after the offending youngman has adequately compensated the father of the bride, or the former husband. The amount decreed by the *panchayat* varies according to the economic position and social status of the parties. In this type of marriage the woman forefeits her claim to the dowry or the *mehr* of her earlier marriage.

By capture: Marriage by capture is a marriage by the use of deception and force. But in Gujar society the term is rather loosely applied to those cases when a real or pretended opposition is made by the friends of the bride when the bridegroom comes to fetch her home. The custom seems to be based upon the belief that a mock fight is a means of repelling evil spirits. Instance of this practice is found among resident Gujars of Chamba, where marriage is a virtual test of valour. Before gaining entry into the bride's village, the groom's marriage party, which comes fore-prepared armed with muzzle-loading guns and sharp shooters, is asked to shoot the target (*taman*) put up at the top of a tall tree, and then to lift a *mugdar*, an enormous club. It is probably a relic of the age-old tradition aimed at ensuring that the bridegroom had the will and the might to protect the bride under all circumstances.[9]

Ceremonies

A marriage is a set of ceremonies conducted at the respective homes of the bride and the groom. Betrothal or engagement is the ceremony which eventually leads to solemnization of marriage. Gujars believe in early betrothal:

5-7 years old sons are often betrothed to girls of 2-4 years in age. 'In the hills it is the father of the boy that sends an envoy to search for a bride for his son' says Lyall in the *Kangra District Land Revenue Settlement Report*. Gujars form no exception to this rule. The negotiations are invariably initiated by the parents of the boy. To select a suitable match is not difficult as among the Hindus. The bride-to-be is most of the time under the very nose of the family, one among many cousin sisters or daughters of near relations. A beautiful, obedient, modest, submissive and an industrious girl, well-versed in household chores undoubtedly is considered an asset. After the family connections, pedigree, *gotra* and customs are found to match, the boy's parents take steps to ascertain informally the willingness of the girl's parents to the union. Both parties indicating their consent, the actual ritual is observed ceremoniously. A few elders visit the girl's house to seek formal consent of her parents and to fix a day for the ceremony, which is held at the bride's place and to which the elders of the community are invited. On the day fixed for the purpose the boy's father accompanied by three elderly relations pays the visit carrying with him certain article of dress, one or two ornaments for the girl and some quantity of *gur, shakar* and ghi. In the presence of the assembly, the boy's father formally asks the girl's father the hand of his daughter for his son and enquires whether the union (*rishta*) is acceptable to him. The father of the girl then replies: 'I assent' or 'I accept this *rishta*'. Some times the question and the answer are repeated three times. Prayer of good will is then recited and is followed with the distribution of *gur* and *shakar* and the community feast. *Shagun* is exchaged by the parties (Rs. 11 to the girl and Re.1 to the boy). The date of marriage as also *haq-i-mahr* are decided on that occasion. Back at his home, the boy's father invites his kith and kin (*nata*) to a feast in order to apprise them of the engagement and to seek the customary approval. Before they disperse, each one of them is made a present of cash generally of Re. 1. They are the ones who then extend invitation to other relatives to join the marriage ceremony.

Once betrothed the boy and the girl and their families start helping each other in each other's transhumant chores. The girl is given gifts on important occasions and festivals and the boy's parents also send presents to her female relatives. The violation of the agreement, say by way of refusing to accept the gifts and presents or by exhibition of behaviour unbecoming of the relationship, often leads to a quarrel, which some times ends in the revocation of the betrothal. The same result would follow if the girl elopes with another youngman or departs this world.

Nikah: Marriage is usually solemnised four to eight years after the betrothal. The various ceremonies connected with it start with *mehndi* or *hennabandi*: both the boy and the girl are anointed with *henna* (*lawsonia alba*). With this is usually combined the rubbing with *haldi* or turmeric. The application of *henna*, saffron and turmeric seems to be, partly a form of initiation, partly protective and stimulating or fertilizing. It is a general custom, perhaps borrowed from the Hindus that the condiments used in the anointing are exchanged between the bride and the bridegroom, a magical device to promote the union of the pair. The girl's hands and the feet are stained with *henna*, her lips with walnut bark, her cheeks rubbed with rouge and her eyes painted with *kajal* (lamp-black). Her hair are washed, oiled with fresh butter and woven into beautiful plaits of the braid. The groom, at his place, is shaved and given the ritual bath. While these rites are being performed, the young girls and ladies sing appropriate marriage songs to the accompaniment of musical instruments and clapping of hands. After the ritual bath both are decked in their wedding dress of pink or yellow colour; the groom by the *maulvi*, who ties the *sehra* (chaplet) also. Of a Gujar groom a stick with a brass handle is an essential part of his dress.

The marriage party (*barat*) comprises of any number of *baratis*, from six, traditionally recommended, to as many as 20/30. Customarily the women donot join the *barat*. Before the procession starts for the bride's place, the groom's mother offers her son a *katora* (cup) of milk; it is considered an auspicious omen. The *barat* is led by musician beating drums; *shehnai* though preferred is however not an essential part of the orchestra. Usually the groom mounts a horse or is seated in a litter but if the distance be not much, he walks on foot alongwith the *baratis*. Fire-works are let off and stick brandishing youngmen dance feverishly. On arrival near their destination, the party is met and greeted either by the father or any other elder relation of the bride. They are then asked to display their valour by shooting at the *taman* and lifting the club, which they call *mugdar* or *mudghar*. It is said that in the days gone-by if the groom's party failed to win the competition, they had to go back of course, in disgrace and without the bride. But now-a-days they become laughing stock of the congregation and abuses are flung at them by the women in their songs. *Milni* is the formal reception. The mother-in-law offers a *dupatta* (a longish piece of fine cloth) to the groom who makes a present (*nazrana*) of some money, generally Rs. 5 to her. The fathers and other close relations of the bride and groom exchange greetings, presents and embrace each other. The stay of the *barat* is made as comfortable as possible and no stone is left unturned by the bride's people to ensure it.

The general name of the marriage service is *nikah*; and no marriage, of whatever form, is considered lawful without this service. According to the Koran and the Traditions marriage depends on three facts: the assent of the parties, the evidence of two witnesses and the marriage settlement. If any of these are wanting, the marriage is considered void. As the auspicious hour approaches, the *maulvi*, appoints two men of full age as witnesses (*vakil*) on the part of the bridegroom; asks them to go to the bride's relations and ask for permission for the *nikah* as also to ascertain the amount of *mehr* or marriage settlement. A *vakil* or an agent of the bride then comes forward to negotiate . At this point there is some mock haggling. According to the Law, the *mehr* consists of two parts: *muajjal*, demandable on entering into the contract and *muwajjal*, which is payable on dissolution of the contract. The former though not claimed at marriage acts as a guarantee of good conduct of the bridegroom, and prevents rash divorce. The *mehr* includes pieces of jewellery and any other moveable or immoveable property. Amongst

Gujars one or more buffaloes or cows besides cash and jewellary are generally pledged as settlement.

When the amount of settlement has been fixed, the *maulvi* ascertains its acceptance by the groom. He then makes him clean his throat three times with water and seating him with his face towards the Mecca makes him repeat the prescribed *ayats* from the *Koran* before reciting the marriage contract. The *vakils* of the bride and the groom join hands and the former says to the latter: 'So and so's daughter, so and so, by the agency of her representatives and the testimony of two witnesses, has, in her marriage with you, had such a settlement made upon her. Do you consent to it?' To this the bridegroom assents and repeats his assent thrice. After the *nikah*, the *maulvi* offers up a prayer on behalf of the couple. He then tells the groom's mother or any other lady to inform the bride that from this day she must consider herself married to so and so. On hearing this the bride weeps or is supposed to weep. On the men's side the bridegroom embraces his friends, kisses their hands and receives congratulations. On their part the musicians strike up a loud, discordant peal as if to scare evil spirits. The friends of the groom and other relation are feasted and then they are ready to return home.

The mother-in-law receives the new bride at the door of her home, places a pot full of milk on her head and details what she has received as *mehr*. The return of the *barat* is followed by a big feast to the kith and kin and neighbourers. Whosoever comes to the feast gives one or two rupees to the bride. By way of *bartan* married sisters of the groom give her as much as one hundred rupees, and in return each one receives a buffalo as *tamol*. This marks the culmination of main festivities as also the formal acceptance of the bride into the family fold. If minor, the bride would go back to her parents and return for consummation of marriage only after she has come of age.

Her dowry[10] (*daz*) usually consists of a couple of ornaments, one or two complete sets of clothes, a light bedding and about half-a-dozen cooking utensils. Some quantity of rice and sugar tied in a piece of coloured cloth is the traditional dowry. In addition a rich father may give her one or two buffaloes. To the groom his in-laws give nothing more than a shirt, a pair of trousers, a jacket and a turban: no ornaments nor any other item of value is presented.

Earlier total expenditure on a marriage used to be between one to four thousand rupees depending upon the means of the family. Now-a-days, however, the trend seems to be to do everything on a lavish scale. That is why it has become one of the main causes of growing indebtedness amongst the Gujars.

The decision is mostly of the parents or relatives: the consent of the boy and the girl is hardly sought. The parents generally donot consider it necessary. A 1985 Study has brought out that only in 20 to 25 per cent of cases they were consulted. Ever since there has been not much of an improvement in the situation. The day a youth would have full freedom to choose a partner looks very far in distant future.

Widow Re-marriage

Among Gujars both junior and senior levitate is in vogue. In essence it is identical with the Jewish levitate. On the death of a man, his younger brother has first claim to marry the widow, failing him, his elder brother. The marriage, however, cannot be performed without the widow's consent. The custom has the double advantage of perpetuating the deceased's name; is economical and saves the family property from division. A Gujar widow with two or more living children normally does not enter into a second wedlock and prefers to retain her rights and to look after and bring up her children. A widow marrying out of family loses all her rights with the sole exception to her dowry. According to the *Koran* a period of probation (*iddat*) must be observed by a divorced wife or a widow before marrying again—three months after divorce and four months and ten days after death of her husband. This form of marriage is performed very simply without any fanfare. The husband throws a wrap (*chadar*) over woman's head and puts bangles on her arms in the presence of the male and female members of his brotherhood.

Divorce

According to the Muslim personal law there are three forms of divorce: revocable within three menstrual periods, the husband saying only once to his wife, 'I have divorced you;' irrevocable unless a second marriage between the parties is performed, the husband repeating the same words twice; and absolute (*talaq-i-mutlaq*), with three similar repetitions. In any event, a divorce to be valid, must be granted by a husband willingly, in full senses and of his free will. In the Gujar community it is the absolute form, which is commonly practised. Usually a man would divorce his wife if she be barren, mentally ill or physically incapacitated or is suspected of extra-marital relationship. A wife may seek it on grounds of incompatibility and the like or if she has eloped with or intends to marry another man.

The family of the husband with intention to divorce his wife summons the *biradari* panchayat and in their presence pronounces the formula of divorce. He picks up three pebbles and while throwing them away one by one every time recites the formula thrice. Thus ends the union and the marriage is legally dissolved. As settlement the divorced wife gets the *mehr* as also her dowry. But if the initiative has come from her, the wife abjures her claim to both of these, *i.e., mehr* and the dowry. Besides, the parents of the woman or the prospective husband, is bound down by the *biradari* to pay compensation to the previous husband.

Death and Death Memorial Services

When the approach of death is imminent, the *maulvi* or in his absence a learned reader of the Koran, recites in a loud voice the Yasin chapter of the Koran. The moment the spirit has fled, the mouth is shut; the eyes are closed and the two great toes are fastened together with a thin strip of cloth. If death occurs late in the night, the shrouding and the burial is done early next morning: the popular belief is that if a good man, he be buried quickly so that he reaches the paradise that sooner, and if a bad man, he should be buried speedily lest his unhappy lot casts a shadow over others. Before shrouding, the corpse is given a bath by some one from amongst the relatives or friends: the parents, wife or husband do not do this duty. The shroud (*kafan*) consists of three pieces of cloth for a man, five for a woman. The biggest or the chief cloth is called the shroud. A shawl or some such covering is thrown over the upper sheet. A Koran is placed at the head of the bier and the body is then ready for interment. The corpse is carefully laid on the shroud cloths, which are invariably white. It is, however, permissible to spread a coloured cloth over the bier (*janaza* or *tabut*) or the coffin (*sanduq*), a square wooden box the length of the corpse, generally manufactured for a *haji*. With the recital of *fatiha* with Qul texts, the body is placed on a bed or bier, or if the family could afford it, in a coffin. Two friends or relatives carry the bier on their shoulders with few others touching it with their hands all the while repeating the creed. Others follow on foot, which is considered a meritorious act. The funeral procession moves at a rapid pace. On arrival at the cemetery the bier is laid down and the service is recited. The service consists of the *Takbir*, the supplication and the prayer for forgiveness. After the service all persons except for relatives and close friends are free to depart. The *fatiha* for the dead is then recited before the bier is raised and taken to the grave-side and body is laid to rest in the pit with head to the north, feet to the south and face towards Mecca. Each person present takes up a little earth and reciting mentally the appropriate Koranic verses, places it on the corpse. The grave is then filled, levelled and a head-stone placed. The grave, which is dug before hand, is large enough to take in the body and four to five feet deep. Some times a side chamber (*lahd*) on the east side of the grave is made to receive the corpse. After the burial *fatiha* is recited in the name of the dead and then repeated in the joint names of all the dead buried in the cemetery when about 40 paces away from the grave. Those last few who accompany the chief mourner back home are generally offered something to drink or eat. It is decreed that the relatives should not weep over-much or go without food: nor is *sijda* (prostration or bowing of head) to the corpse permissible. The women do not join the funeral party nor wail or beat their breasts in mourning.

Among the Gujars the rites known as *tija, viz.*, visit to and the flower offering at the grave called *ziyarat* is not performed. This they observe on the seventh day and call it *sata*. On the morning of this day the grave is visited and flowers are placed on it. There is recitation from the Koran and alms are given to the poor and the *faqirs*. In the evening a feast is hosted and those invited come along with some grains, ghi for the family and also give some money to the heir or the widow. She also receives a few pieces of utensils from the very close relations. *Fatiha* is recited before the food is partaken, a part of which is distributed among the poor. All these days recitation from the Koran continues and some people are known to light every evening a lamp at the grave.

On the morning of the fortieth day, *ziyarat* is made to the grave and friends and relatives are given a feast. This day a goat is slaughtered and meat is served for the first time after the death. Among Gujars of Chamba, *ladoos* made of maize atta is a delicacy served with rice and meat, the latter two, a common menu every where else. With the *chaliya* the mourning for the departed soul comes to an end; though for three subsequent years on the day of death, alms are given and prayers said in the name of the deceased.

Regarding utilization of services of a *maulvi* in these ceremonies, a definite attitudinal change has, of late, been noticed. It finds reflection in the following Table.

Table 5.1: Attitudinal Change in the Utilization of Services of a *Maulvi*

Response At birth	No. of respondents		Response At circumcision	No. of respondents
Yes	202	(67.33)	Yes	256 (85.33)
No	55	(18.33)	No	44 (14.67)
No response	43	(14.34)	No response	00 (00.00)
	300	(100)		300(100.00)
At engagement/ marriage			At death, chaliha etc.	
Yes	274	(91.33)	Yes	300(100.00)
No	26	(8.67)	No	00 (0.00)
No response	00	(0.00)	No response	00 (0.00)

(Figures in *parantheses* indicate percentage).

It is remarkable to note that failure to utilise the services of *maulvi* has been attributed solely to economic reasons. The trend shows that for reason of poverty, the Gujars are drifting away from their socio-religious mores. It also portends that as the time passes this tendency is likely to spread at a wider scale, and not always for want of money.

Notes and References

1. Crooke, William, *Islam in India—The Customs of the Musalmans of India*; Oxford University Press, 1921; Reprint New Delhi, 1972.

2. Molinowski, B., *Argonauts of the Western Pacific* (cited by Nag D.S. in *Tribal Economy*), Delhi, 1958.

3. Rose, H.A., *A Glossary of the Tribes and Castes of the Punjab & North-west Frontier Province*, Vol. III; 1883 Reprint, New Delhi, 1982.

4. Bingley, A.H., History, Caste and Culture of Jats and Gujars; 1899, Reprint New Delhi, 1978.

5. Rose, H.A., *A Glossary of the Tribes & Castes*, op cit.

6. Singh, K.S. (Ed.), *People of India: Himachal Pradesh*, Vol. XXIV; New Delhi, 1996.

7. Crooke, William, *Islam in India*, op cit.

8. Musalmans are allowed by the Koran and the Traditions to have four wives. 'One quarrels with you, two are sure to involve you in their quarrels; when you have three factions are formed against her you love best; but four find society and occupation among themselves, leaving the husband in peace.' (Crooke William: *Islam in India*).

9. Handa O.C., 'Where marriage is a test of valour' *The Tribune*, 14th Jan, 1968. Also see. Singh, R.C. (Ed), *Maingal: a Village Survey* Census of India, 1961, Vol. XX, Part VI No. 27, New Delhi , 1964.

10. The dowry remains the property of the bride so long as she lives. If she dies childless her nearest relatives can reclaim it, but if she leaves children they take it. It must be distinguished from the settlement (*mehr*) made by husband on his wife.

6

Transhumance—Responses of Migration

Drama of Transhumance

'The drama of herding and migration; the idleness of a pastoral existence, where the herds satisfy the basic needs of men, and most of one's labour is expended on travelling and maintaining a minimum of personal comfort, and hardly any of it is productive in any obvious sense, the freedom of necessity of movement through a vast, barren and beautiful landscape. . . all these things assume a growing aesthetic and moral importance as one participates in nomadic life.' Observes Frederick Bath in his study of Bass, a nomadic tribe of Persia.[1] These features, common to *Ban*-Gujars, are, however, strikingly unfamiliar to members of sedentary society.

The *Ban*-Gujars are buffalo rearing pastoral nomads who transhume from alpine pastures of Himachal Pradesh down to the lower Siwaliks and the plains of the Punjab and as far down as the districts of Saharanpur and Dehradun in Uttar Pradesh. Their pastoral economy is totally dependent upon the availability and exploitation of natural pastures, which are markedly seasonal in occurrence. During winter when the Himalayan ranges wear the thick snow mantle, the pasturage in the lower Siwalik ranges and the valleys holds out a tempting invitation to them. As summer approaches and the fodder in the lower reaches dries up, grazing grounds in the higher reaches come alive no sooner the snow begins to thaw. That is whereto the Gujars with their herds then start the trek, repeating the process of transhumance year after year: the sole motivating force pushing them on to reach areas where the grass is fresh, green and luxuriant to provide good and nutritious fodder and wholesome water from the gurgling streams or gushing springs to their herds of animals. Over the years each family has followed well-defined tracks from winter grazing grounds to the *dhars* in alpine meadows and *vice-versa* going over high mountain passes, fording numerous bubbling streams and foaming rivers with some families traversing two to three hundred kilometres each way. From these traditional routes, the Gujars do not usually deviate because with the routes they follow they have, over the time, become quite familiar and so have their animals. The topography of the areas they pass through, and of its climate and weather conditions they have since become conversant with. They know the people and they are well assured of ample fodder and water for their animals as also of markets to purchase necessaries of life and to dispose of their milk produce at or near the halting places. These advantages and conveniences mostly out-weigh any thought of switching over to any new and unknown track. Across these tracks they have, over the years, developed a set plan of seasonal migration; the timing of departure; places of halt and the eventual destination. Only when their grazing areas are closed or shifted by the Forest Department, they, of necessity, venture to make appropriate changes in their time-honoured pattern.

Seasonal Rhythm of Migration

The Gujars plan their activities into four major segments of time, *viz.,* winter, spring, summer and autumn. During their annual transhumance they occupy different altitudinal zones or localities in succession in different seasons while shifting from winter to summer pastures and *vice-versa*: the two most pronounced time-cycles of mass movement occurring in spring and again in autumn. These transhumants progressively shift their animals keeping in view the climatic tolerance of the animals and the optimum utilization of available pastures between altitude-defined climatic zones. They take their animals to the areas where pasturage is available in abundace and which is simultaneously free from detrimental climatic extremes. This pattern of migration is universal and the annual cycle of transhumant activities is a matching response to the seasonal rhythm of annual behavioral pattern in its temporal spread over space. During the hot weather, the Gujars drive their herds to the upper ranges, where the buffaloes rejoice in the rich grasses which spring up during the rains, and at the same time attain condition from the temperate climate and the immunity from the venomous flies which torment their existence in the plains. And in the cold weather they are found grazing the cattle in the woods and the lower reaches of the river basins.

State of Transhumance

A *dera* generally comprises of ten to fifteen families, though small ones of only 2-3 families marching in a single formation are not an uncommon sight: the bigger ones move in two or three groups, one following the other at 2-3 days' interval. These groups march daily and cover mostly short but on certain stretches long distances till they reach the intervening pastures, where they may relax for about 7-10 days socially mixing with members of other *deras*.

On the long journey there are certain tension zones. Factors like uncertain and un-predictable weather conditions, accident prone trail, hostility of the local farmers, fear of wild animals and the like account for early start, long march and late-night camping. Social causes such as birth or death and economic necessity to visit market towns lead to halts of two to three nights. A prolonged halt of a week or ten days is made primarily to utilize the intervening pastures.

The mid-April heat of the plains or the initial chill of winter in September ignites restlessness not only in men but is evidenced in the behaviour of Gujars' animals as well. Both the man and the beast senses that time has come to make the move and accordingly preparations are set afoot. These preparations, of necessity, have to be made on somewhat elaborate scale. All the dirty linen is washed clean; torn and worn out bedding and wearing apparel is mended and repaired; large utensils and other house-hold goods are packed in gunny bags of appropriate size and load and made ready to be carried by pack animals, ponies or bulls. Salt, pepper, chillies and other condiments are ground and stocked in small cloth bags or tins and so are the tea leaves, sugar, jaggery and numerous herbs and medicinal seeds and leaves for the men and the animals. Similarly a small quantity of flour and pulses are purchased, cleaned and packed for use at *paraos* situated far from market-place.

Three or four days before the day considered auspicious by the *maulvi* to start the march, *khatam* is held in order to ensure a smooth and trouble-free journey. This rite is a community affair in which all the members of the *dera* join and led by the *maulvi* offer prayers. *Fatiha* is recited over *khir* (rice cooked in sweetened milk) and *halwa* (pudding), which is then distributed among all those present on the occasion.

Normally a *dera* starts the march by late morning. Rising early the buffaloes and cows are milked, grazed for a while; camp is broken, packing and loading is done, all before nine or ten A.M. When in close proximity of a town, they try to sell the milk yield of the previous evening as also of the morning, often at relatively cheap rate. Other-wise rather than carrying and spoiling, it is turned into cottage cheese or *khoya*. In tension-free zones they do not cover much distance, usually between 10 and 15 kms., and by 3-4 P.M. they camp for the night sparing enough daylight to graze and feed the cattle as also for lopping nearby trees for night feed. On the other hand when passing through difficult stretches with long journey ahead, they rise early, do rapid packing and loading within 15-30 minutes and rush ahead without any dalliance on the way sometimes covering a distance of twenty to thirty kilometres in a single day. The pattern of their seasonal movement—nature of daily marches and duration of halts—, in short, has a strong corelation with the seasonal land-use of the migration routes. The character of the approach routes limit the outer parameters of their onward and return movements: these are not simple back and forth routine movements set by calendar. In fact the distance of each day's march, selection of halting site, and duration of stay at a particular point in different topographical zones are factors dependent mainly upon the basic needs of the flock, *viz.*, availability of good pasturage, avoidance of undue fatigue, loss from natural hazards and conflict with the local *zamindars* as also performance of a few sedentary activities on the migratory routes. That is how their stay for several days in those zones which provide most advantageous conditions for their herds is explained. In less favourable tracts they are chary to stay for more than a single night.

As earlier stated the day of departure starts early both for men and the women. All are up much before sun-rise. While the men attend to the herd, milk the milch animals and break the camp, the women brew tea and roast *chapatis*, with some extra for the children, the old and the weak, to be eaten before the next meal is cooked at the next halting place. Packing is done both by men and the women. The first to make the move are the men and the animals. They are followed by pack animals laden with all the house-hold baggage including beddings and tents. On top of the luggage, sit, well secured, the children of the *dera* who are too young to walk long distances. The women, the old and the infirm alongwith weak and sick livestock forms the rear-guard marching in charge of an experienced and mature lady. Other women walk alongside balancing on their heads, the loads of utensils packed in rope-nets or milk or milk products with a stout staff in the right hand. Even small children contribute their mite by carrying either a hen or a cock or something else. Infants are carried by young mothers slung on their backs and newly-born calves by the Gujars on their shoulders while the watch dogs keep a vigil over the entire moving caravan.

Soon after arrival at the place of halt, the women unpack the luggage. The next thing they attend to is putting up a make-shift cooking fire-place. A small depression is dug into the ground selected for the kitchen and around it are placed a few stones to give them the shape and form of a common Indian *chulha* (cooking fire-place). Not all the women apply mud mortar to the stones. With dry branches, drift wood and withered bushes collected from the nearby forest by the women and children, fire is lit and some of the women start preparing mid-day meal. One or two Gujars go to the nearest village or town to look for hay or dry maize stalks to feed their cattle. Once the source has been located, all other families are informed and each one purchases as per their individual requirements. In the meantime the buffaloes, cows, bulls, sheep or goats browse and graze in the nearby waste land or forest. The lunch is mostly of maize *chapatis*, which are eaten with small quantity of ghi, salt and ground chillies applied to one side. In the press of time cooking of *dal* or vegetable is out of question. After the meal is over, the cattle are taken to the nearby stream or spring to water and graze. Some times one or two Gujars would take the cattle to the nearby pasture even before the lunch, which their women-folk would later fetch for them. After they have taken the meals, cleaned and scoured the utensils, the women have some spare time to carry on other house-hold activities like rope making or for their toilette like washing, lousing and braiding their hair. Soon it is tea time and time to gather some more fire-wood for the evening and next morning. The evening meal is no different from the lunch except that some families might cook some *dal* or some leafy vegetable gathered from the nearby stream or forest. The men bring back the herd, tether them and give night feed especially to the milch-cattle lest they dry up the milk. The milch cows and buffalo are milked and the milk is boiled by the women in several vessels and stored over-night for sale next morning. Some families sour some to make curd for self-consumption and sale. Very often one or two men of a family would visit the market next morning to sell milk or curd. They join the *dera* later at or near about the next camp. Such of them who have no spare hand to market the milk will give it to some other Gujar brother for sale on their behalf. With the fading of day light, the family is ready to go to bed. Whatever bedding they have, they unpack and spread on the bare ground around their luggage and close to their herd of cattle. Fire is kept burning all through the night with a view to scare wild animals. Besides, the dogs are there to keep the night watch.

Gujars are a thoroughly integrated community and co-operate with each other to be best of their capability.

Neighbour pitches in to help neighbour. If any family runs short of anything essential, others would readily and cheerfully come forward to share their stock. If there is a birth, death, illness or accident, even strangers would rush to do whatever possibly they could to mitigate the distress. When a Gujar intends visiting the market, he would invariably enquire from other families if he could bring anything for them. Normally a *dera* starts march together: all the families wait with great patience till everyone is ready to move. Borrowing or lending of money within the community is common. What is remarkable is that the transaction is *sans* consideration and this attribute is highly conducive to their economy and solvency.

Traditional Routes

The *padaos* or halting points are generally the same old places selected for their favourable situation; proximity to the main roads; not far from a village or town nor too near to village fields and where water and fodder for the animals is easily available. Instead of keeping to the main roads, as they generally do, some Gujar families prefer routes along streams and rivers because of abundance of water and fodder for their cattle. In any case they elect to follow such routes which are convenient, less risky and, in transition cheaper in terms of fodder cost.

The important routes the *Ban*-Gujars have traditionally followed and the focal points at which they make small halts on the long march are[2]:

Chamba Forest Circle

Route I - Tissa/Tikri-Pukhri-Chamba-Bathri-Nainikhad-Dhunera-Chakki. Pathankot (Punjab).

Major places of halt:- Pukhri, Chamba, Bathri, Nainikhad, Dhunera, Bakhtpur, Dhar, Chakki, Mamoon, Pathankot/Gurdaspur.

Route II - Sahoo-Chamba bridge-Nurpur-Chakki-Pathankot.

Major places of halt: Chamba bridge, Chaurikhas, Nurpur, Chakki, Pathankot/Gurdaspur.

Route III - Sahoo-Chowari-Nurpur-Mamoon-Pathankot.

Major places of halt:- Mirdi, Mangla, Karer, Jote, Chowari, Katsasni, Nurpur, Nagawari, Mamoon, Pathankot/Gurdaspur.

Route IV - Bhandal (Sangni)-Bathri-Dhunera-Dhar-Gurdaspur (Pb).

Major places of halt:-Saraga, Salooni, Sundla, Brungal, Bathri, Nainikhad, Dhunera, Bakhtpur, Dhar, Chakki, Pathankot/Gurdaspur.

Focal points: Bathri, Dhunera, Dhar, Chamba and Chauri .khas.

Shimla Forest Circle:

Route I - Kotgarh-Kotkhai-near Solan-Ambala/Patiala.

Major places of halt:- Bagi, Kotkhai, near Solan. Punjab/Haryana.

Route II - Kotgrah-Kotkhai-near Rajgrah-Majra-Nahan.

Major places of halt:- Bagi, Kotkhai, Habban, Rajgarh, Dadahu, Majra/Nahan.

Route III - Rohru-Tharoch-Dehradun.

Major places of halt:- Country road, Tharoch, Dehradun.

Route IV - Chopal-Dehradun/Nahan.

Major places of halt:- Country road, Dehradun/Nahan.

Route V - Shimla-near Chail-Solan-Nalagrah-Ropar.

Major places of halt:- Near Chail-Solan-Saini-Majra-Nalagarh-Ropar.

Focal points: Solan, Majra, Balag.

Nahan Forest Circle:

Route I - Rajgarh-Renuka-Nahan/Majra.

Major places of halt:- Renuka, Dadahu, Nahan/Majra.

Route II - Haban-near Rajgarh-Nahan/Majra.

Major places of halt:- Khera dhar, near Rajgarh/Dadahu, Nahan/Majra.

Focal points: Dadahu and Majra.

Kullu Forest Circle:

Route I - Hurla-Bhuntar-Jogindernagar.

Major places of halt:- Bhuntar, Chharaur, Mali, Barog, Jogindernagar.

Route II - Parbati-Bhuntar- Barog-Jogindernagar.

Major places of halt:- Bhuntar, Chharaur, Mali, Barog, Jogindernagar.

Route III - Manali-Kullu-Mandi.

Major places of halt:- Kullu, Bajaura, Bathri, Mandi.

Route IV - Naggar-Kullu-Mandi.

Major places of halt: Kullu, Bajaura, Bathri, Mandi.

Route V - Banjar-Ani-Solan-Punjab/Haryana.

Major Places of halt:- Ani, Tattapani, Halog, near Solan, Punjab/Haryana.

Focal points : Bhuntar and Bajaura.

Camping Places

Who decides where to make the halt, the site the camp is to be made at and whether it is of some advantage to camp near a town or any other small population certre? A random survey has shown that in the view of half of them the question is meaningless because they have been halting and camping at the same old places year after year. One fourth of those who responded, however, said that it is the *kafila* or *dera* leader who makes the choice bearing in mind the overall interest of the caravan. And more than 60 per cent expressed preference for halts in the vicinity of a township or any reasonably large village. The main considerations which weigh in favour of the choice, according to them, are ready availability of fodder for the cattle, better chance they have to sell the milk and milk products and the convenience in effecting minor purchases of food articles and other necessaries of life.

Social Problems

The deep rooted institution of transhumance and its influence in moulding social and economic milieu of the Gujar community is a thing of the past. Gone are the days when *Ban*-Gujars were invited guests of the princes, and free souls grazing their herds where they willed with no restriction as to how many cattle they kept. The present regulatory system, an imposition of the State, with the object to preserve and conserve the natural resource of alarmingly dwindling forest cover through its ever-rising stringency, is eliminating their age-old life style with obvious deleterious effect on their social and economic condition. No wonder caught in the poverty trap they are going downhill.

No one can fault the State policy. But it is palpably inequitable to assert that their right of grazing is 'not of the nature as the rights of *zamindars*.'[3] On top of it comes the large-scale arbitrariness in the issue or renewal of permits; a long-standing grouse of the community. There is over-crowding and diminution in the quality of the pastures. Grazing on the silly by un-authorised persons including local and migratory graziers, no doubt with the connivance of low-level officials, all are playing havoc with the tribe's peace of mind and their conscience. The repetitive shifting of ground is further causing untold physical misery and mental torture to them as also to their cattle. An analysis[4] conducted on the basis of data collected in the course of a field survey revealed that over the study period of ten years (1950-60) only 30 per cent of the Gujar families were fortunate enough to be allowed entry to the old pastures year after year. Almost half of them had to change two to five different pastures and 15 per cent between six to nine. It is significant to note that around 5 per cent of them were tossed about around ten or even more grazing areas. Put in other words, 70 per cent of the Gujar families were denied security of tenure and had to face totally new environment every year or in alternate or third year, just to eke out a meagre living. It is an experience which neither the man nor the beast cherishes. The position has not improved since nor is there any hope.

Among nomadic Gujars there are families who transhume within a very limited area passing the summer as also winter at different altitudes of the same Forest Division. Such families are not many. They rather form an exception to the rule. There are others, estimated to be around 10%, whose sphere of movement covers more than one Forest Circle, not necessarily located adjacent to each other. The majority, however, is formed by those who migrate from their summer alpine pastures situated in the remote pockets of the State to the distant plains of Punjab and Uttar Pradesh.

The study[5] which encompassed 65 Gujar families summer-camping in three Forest Ranges of Bamta, Upper Pabar and Tranda, concentrated in an area of 25-30 kilometres surrounding the urban centres of Kotkhai, Jubbal and Rohru and the small township of Sarahan in Rampur sub-division, revealed that the actual period spent in migration varied from family to family depending chiefly on the distance each one had to cover from and back to its summer grazing area. Analytically speaking, a very negligible number of *deras*—less than 5 per cent—spent around a fortnight in transit; while 25 per cent of them had to make the trek over 15-30 days with another 25 per cent faced the ordeal for 31-59 days. Significantly half of the families remained in travel status for two to three months every year.

Continuous travel for months together gives birth to some social and health problems. The women who are in family way, in the circumstance, are denied privacy and deprived of the right of medical care. They have no shelter above their heads and in case of any labour complication, death of the mother or the child or of both, becomes inevitable unless the family manages to carry her in time to a well-equipped health centre. Such cases are neither negligible in number nor take place in rare and exceptional circumstances. On the other hand these are everyday occurrences taking place in the backwoods. Incidentally the study referred to above, revealed that in the 65 subject families, 78 mothers gave birth to 318 children and of these as many as 93 or 29.2 per cent were born while the *dera* was on the migratory trail. It would have been of great social interest had Mr. Jistu gone deeper to find out as to how many of these unfortunate young mothers survived the ordeal. Without doubt, not all of them would have survived without mental trauma or physical damage. Among the new-borns, the mortality rate, he found alarmingly high at 34.6 per cent; 42.7 per cent died within one year of birth and 46.4 per cent before they had seen five summers of curable diseases like diarrhoea and measles. Of the tender souls, Jistu found, 23.6 per cent embraced premature death solely for lack of maternity care services and another 15.5 per cent because of trial and tribulations of migration. This, in short, is shown in Table 6.1, which elucidates the dismal picture:-

Table 6.1: Child mortality and causes

	No. of deaths	Percentage to the total
Below one year	47	42.7
Between 1 to 2 years	32	29.1
Between 3 to 5 years	19	17.3
Over 5 years	12	10.9
	110	100.0
Main causes of death:		
Lack of maternity care	26	23.6
Migration	17	15.5
Various diseases including		
Malnutrition	67	60.9

It generally does not cause any concern or surprise to know that buffaloes and cows too calve in similar circumstances. Though unable to express their pain, they without doubt, too undergo much suffering because of fatigue, hunger and other hardships of the long and arduous journeys. It has been noted that in their case the percentage of calving whilst on the move is equally significant. Of the 1014 calves born as many as 235 (22.6%) were shown to have been born in this condition, and majority of them, which incidentally were mostly male, did not survive.

The nomadic Gujars by and large follow the traditional system of medicine, both for themselves and their animals, which mainly revolves round herbs growing in the wild. It is a circumstance not of their free choice as access to any public health centre or veterinary institution is limited. No mobile or peripatetic health-care institution serves them in the fastness of their summer camps or wide-spread winter grazing areas. The system is not just *hocus pocus*. Instead it is based on deep pharmacological knowledge acquired over centuries and passed by one generation to the next. Learning by experience the head of every family in time becomes proficient in treating routine cases of diseases and ailments both of men and the animals. However in more serious cases the Gujars would consult the *sayana*, the wise old man. The secret of the skill lies in a fair knowledge of herbal medicines as also an expertise in setting broken bones. Even now-a-days there are a couple of them to whom patients from far and wide including non-tribals turn seeking cure. In one of them, the cancer patients in particular have reportedly great faith. Much before the pharmaceutical laboratories started extracting *Di-acetyl-baccatine*, an alkaloid from *Taxus baccata*, locally called *Brahmi* or *Rakhal* tree, the traditional Gujar doctors have been brewing some potion from its leaves to successfully treat many forms of cancer. Incidentally when tea leaves be not available, the Gujar women would brew the leaves of the same tree to make their everyday tea.

It would, however, be wrong to assume that their attitude to modern medicine is hostile or luke-warm. On the contrary they have been observed to be quite keen to benefit from it. A shade more than 88 per cent of the nomadic Gujars were recently found[6] admitting that they have faith in these sciences and they are more than satisfied with the treatment they have had occasion to avail of whilst in the plains or near towns. It was an insignificant minority of them, say one of every ten persons interviewed, who showed faith in the traditional system of medicine. What all of them keenly wish is that modern facilities should be available to them at their door step whether during migration or in summer camping grounds. More than one-third of those contacted cited the cost of treatment and medicines prohibitive and beyond their means and so wished it to be delivered free of cost.

Jistu's study stretching over one year and covering the sixty-five families, subject of his research, revealed that malaria felled 59.6 per cent of the families; 13.8 per cent sufferred from pneumonia; 9.3 per cent from typhoid and 20 per cent from other diseases and body injuries. In their case the bout of an illness generally lasted longer than usual mainly because they do not have the advantage of modern medical system and so mostly depended on their traditional methods of treatment or in despair turned to charms and witch-craft. A few of them often purchase commonly known tablets like Anacin, Aspro, Sulphadiazine or the like sold over the counter by petty shopkeepers in villages. Only when a patient turns really serious they think of taking him to a hospital or dispensary. Consequently it takes longer than usual to cure. Jistu's survey showed that in 49.2% of families the incidence of illness lasted upto 15 days; in 32.2% instances, between 15 to 29 days and in remaining 18.5% of cases it prolonged beyond 30 days.

When asked whether they preferred modern or traditional system of treatment when their cattle fell ill, 22 persons gave no response, 74 or 24.67% favoured modern treatment and as large a number as 204 constituting 68% of the total respondents (300) showed inclination towards traditional methods.[7] It clearly brings out that faith in their centuries-old practices is still dominant with them. The obvious reason for this trend could be that veterinary institutions in close proximity of their summer or winter camps have not been opened by the government. Higher cost of treatment may also be another inhibiting factor.

Raison d'etre

For the sake of bare sustenance *Ban*-Gujars undergo untold sufferings. One may thus wonder why they continue moving inspite of penury, the tough life, the bleak future of their children and in the process totally depriving themselves of the comforts of the settled life. The answer is not far to find. It lies in the stark fact that they have no other skill nor education to take up any other vocation. Dairying is what their ancestors practised and it is the trade they perforce have to carry on, homeless and landless[8] as they are. They have no roots nor attachment to any particular place. One anecdote about the Gujars goes that once during cross-examination, a Gujar, who was appearing as a witness in the conspiracy case against Sheikh Abdullah in 1959, was asked whether he was loyal to India or Pakistan. Pat came his reply: 'I am loyal to none but my buffalo'![9] Further more the very nature of the profession compels him not to stay continuously at one place but to transhume between alpine pastures and the plains and valleys. It is what they feel and what in reality is the truth. Reaction of more than three-fourth of those who responded to the query as to why do they migrate was that they do so because of climatic compulsions and in search of fodder for their cattle.

Grazing Policy

In pre-Independence India, the territory presently named Himachal Pradesh, was in part administered as an integral part of the province of Punjab and most of the hill country was ruled by numerous petty quasi-autonomous princes. Human settlement in the region was sparse mostly concentrated in river valleys. Even at present the population of the State is overwhelmingly rural totally dependent upon agriculture and related activities including rearing of livestock which continues to be the chief source of livlihood next only to agriculture. Before the economic devel pment motivated by the imperial interests set in, the Himalayan forests were exploited lightly. Grazing land was far more extensive than the needs of its limited live-stock population. Certain rights for use of the forest produce and grazing were conferred as appendage to the cultivated land assessed to land revenue. Vast areas of mountain land remained unutilised and the rulers preserved them as their personal hunting grounds. The role of the State in regulating the livestock economy and extracting a modest income from it was in real terms embedded in the unique system of live-stock ecology in the region.

For centuries the live-stock in the State has had three major components. The non-migratory domestic animals kept by the land-owning peasantry grazed in village waste lands, unclassed forests, demarcated and undemarcated forests, and sometimes even in reserved forests in exercise of the rights recorded in the revenue and forest Settlements. The second and rather commercial segment comprises of migratory graziers, who stay in their homes for a limited period only and migrate to other places with their flocks of sheep and goats in search of seasonal pastures. For the greater part of the year they are on the move in alpine ranges during the summer and in low hills scrub areas in the winter. Nomadic graziers, the third component, have no hearth or home within the territory of the State. They either hail from places outside the State or rather belong to no place in particular, and keep on moving around with their animals from place to place throughout the year. Of them *Ban*-Gujars are numerous than others like Khampas, Bhots, Lahulas etc. *Ban*-Gujars are a purely pastoral race owning large herds of buffaloes. They also own a very limited number of ponies, cows, bullocks and a few sheep and goats. Their spread throughout the State has been necessitated by gradual increase in their population and the ever-rising need of seeking new pastures for their herds growing progressively in number. Some of them have since acquired petty land-holdings not so much to eke out a living from the pursuit of agriculture but rather to acquire rights in pasturage which, on the basis of land or forest Settlements, go with the landed estates.

In the merging pricely States by and large no limit was applied to local or foreign cattle which could graze in the forests outside closed areas, with the inevitable result that huge flocks of migratory graziers and nomadic Gujars could graze in the low hills of the States during winter and in alpine pastures during summer. There was virtually no control except for restrictions of grazing on such bits which were closed for regeneration purposes. In the rest of the area un-restricted grazing of all kinds of animals was allowed on payment of nominal fee. By the time Himachal Pradesh was formed the ravages caused by the uncontrolled and indiscriminate grazing had already made a sordid appearance.

The Western Himalaya is characterised by the peculiar practice of nomadic grazing. The poor soil fertility, sloping lands, lack of irrigation and primitive methods of cultivation render agricultural productivity to bare subsistence level. That is why the meagre income from agriculture was in the past and still continues to be supplemented by the practice of animal husbandry. For the poor people it has been the obvious choice because the steep hills here provide good grazing lands besides the rich pastures in the high alpine areas and numerous low hills which are suitable for winter grazing. The migratory system, which once was eco-

sustained is now subject of devastating resource pressure and the eco-socio-economic rupturing of the migratory grazing system *vis-a-vis* the preservation of forest wealth has assumed the form of a crisis situation. According to experts, over-grazing, excessive extraction of fuelwood and herbs, unscientific lopping of trees for fodder, and forest fires are some of the factors contributing to the shrinking forest cover of the State. It is a complex problem defying satisfactory solution and right from its formation, Himachal Pradesh has been facing it without much success. Soon after its inception, the then Administration appointed B.S. Pramar, an officer of the Indian Forest Service, to go into the grazing problems of the State and after detailed and intensive survey of grazing conditions, to make recommendations for meeting the demands of the graziers consistent with the conservancy and the scientific management of the forests. In his report[10] Parmar pinpointed the source of greatest damage to the forests and other vegetation to the buffalo herds of nomadic Gujars and the roving flocks of sheep and goats of migratory graziers. In fact the report mainly blamed the Gujars for the 'appalling conditions' in which forests in general are 'at present' (1959). In paragraph 29 of his report Parmar draws a grim picture of what he termed as the 'devastating situation'. In his words:

> The animals of the Gujars are *as notoriously* destructive to the growth and conservancy of forests as the migratory flocks are. The damage done to the vegetation by the buffaloes is universally known and acknowledged. The bufalloes are very much more exacting than the kine. Their greater demand for fodder leads to serious decrease in grass production. With their heavy hoofs they trample down the ground and on steep slopes cause sheet erosion and give rise to ravines. Herds of these buffaloes are taken to the alpine ranges in summer and are brought down in winter. Not only do they graze in the alpine pastures but through out the high lying undemarcated forests where much damage is done both by lopping and heavy grazing. The damage

done by these herds to the forests enroute while going up or coming down from alpine pastures is in no way less exacting.

In a later iteration of the official assessment, the words *as notoriously* used by Parmar came to be substituted by the words 'more notoriously' exhibiting pronounced bias against the water buffalo.

The causes which have led to the present 'deplorable state of affairs', Parmar attributed to 'large scale felling of forest tracts outside reserved and demarcated protected forests' which has taken place 'in an unrestricted manner for house construction, for the extension of cultivation and for finding grazing grounds for the ever-increasing cattle.' 'These fellings', the report suggested, 'combined with fires, lopping and over-grazing has resulted in the destruction of large forests and grazing areas'. To combat the grave situation, he advised a sound forest management policy to be put in position so that the forest wealth could be worked and maintained under sound scientific management principles and grazing could be restricted to only that much of cattle and flocks which the soil could support without any grave harm or injury to this natural resource. Parmar's solution was a package of strategies like raising substantially the tax level; correct enumeration and registration of herds and flocks and strict control over their movement. Taking a cue form the guidelines enshrined in the Constitution, he had further suggested, the initiation of suitable measures aimed at improving the quality of livestock as also of fodder and grass lands.

In an exercise to match the available pasture land with the then existing livestock population, he came across a disproportionally vast gap between the two, his calculation showing more than 50% of the cattle population in excess of the number that could be supported by the available pasture lands. Incidentally Parmar had relied on the cattle Census Table contained in the Forest Department Administration Report for the year 1949-50. It showed the cattle population at 19,48,336, considerably less than what the Census taken by the Revenue Department had depicted in 1950-51. By 1987 the livestock population of the State had sky-rocketed to 54,67,516 or 52,62,704 as per the subsequent census of 1992. In percentage terms the proliferation has been to a mind-boggling extent of 270%. From it one thing is obvious. Far from reducing the livestock declared surplus by Parmar, the State has miserably failed to control its growth.

Another instrument of policy recommended by Parmar related to imposition of a high dose of taxation, an indirect way to achieve reduction in cattle population. For this purpose he had proposed grouping the three distinct categories namely, local, special and foreign and levying different rates of grazing fee on each one. Regarding *Ban*-Gujars, 'the solution' he opined 'lies not in the extinction of the buffaloes, but preventing their grazing on slopes either eroding or liable to erode; in reducing their number to the fodder-capacity of their grazing grounds and in regulating the lopping'. Towards that end he suggested the heaviest tax on buffaloes, *i.e.*, Rs.10 per head for foreign grazing; additional fee of same amount for special grazing, and, if local grazing too was availed of an extra levy of Rs. 6. The necessary implication of the proposal meant that a Gujar who was a bonafide resident of a village or locality could graze his cattle in the *bartan* area on payment of local grazing fee like any other *zamindar*. But if he grazed the cattle outside of it but within the limits of the same Forest Division, he was liable to pay for special grazing as well. Grazing in a Forest division of which he be not a resident constituted 'foreign grazing' entailing additional payment for it. The core of the proposal *vis-a-vis Ban*-Gujars was that every family had to pay three fees annually: one for the winter pasture, a second on migration and a third for alpine summer grazing rights. Parmar's proposals further heightened the graziers' opposition to governmental restrictions and the higher fees which he had proposed were not imposed. It was only recently, to be precise, in the year 1972 that the Government eventually raised[11] the grazing charges but at much lower scale than suggested by Parmar. On buffaloes instead of levying independent charges for the three different types of grazing, a unified[12] fee was prescribed at the rate of Rs.8 per annum for each head of cattle.

In 1966 the State Government organized a meeting at Bilaspur where its representatives and the shepherds agreed to reduce the percentage of goats in the flocks. But the following year the government dropped out and instead proposed only to reduce the permissible number of goats by 20%. Under the deteriorating political compulsions another commission[13] was established; this one more sympathetic to the shepherds. The Commission found it very difficult to propose politically viable strategies. It re-iterated that the fees on goats as well as on the rapidly rising population of water buffalo should be raised. Beyond this it could suggest little chiefly in the absence of reliable and adequately detailed data on the livestock and grazing resources. On most major issues the Commission proposed an intensive five year effort to gather systematic data while existing management system remained unchanged. Since then no major Commission has been formed and indeed the existing system has continued to function largely as before.

Alongwith other cattle, the water buffalo too got a temporary reprieve as there was 'to be no compulsory decrease in their number till 1975' when the exercise recommended by the high level Committee was to be completed. In the ultimate analysis, however, the Gujars were denied a place in the grazing scene of the State by the Grazing Advisory Committee. Receiving the maximum blame at its hands for damaging the forest growth and land in high hills, the Gujars were destined to be permanently settled 'in well planned colonies like Aurangabad in Nahan Forest division' and of buffalo grazing there was to be 'complete elimination in large in the open by 2000 A.D' in an annually phased programme. Apparently the Committe had not taken into consideration consequential side-effects like likely adverse impact on the economy of the community as also of the State. T.S. Negi, who too was a member of the Committee, later expressed concern in this regard. Alluding to Gujars' buffaloes, he says[14]:

> It is seriously questionable whether the insistence on the reduction of the numbers is at all sound

policy. Milk and milk products will continue to be more and more in demand for all foreseeable future. Even with rapid strides in the improvement of breeds, will reduction in number be at all wise, seeing that the strides of the Malthusian formula of increase in human population continue to be even more rapid? Will it not be the right thing to do if, instead, feeding resources in a settled economy are improved alongside rapid improvement in breeds and numbers left to look after themselves within that framework?

Incidence of Gujar Grazing

Forests play a vital role in the economy of the *Ban*-Gujars. They mainly depend on them for grazing of their animals. And this they cannot do without proper authorisation of the Department of Forest Farming and Conservation. The permits, which incidentally, are inherited by sons on the demise of their fathers, have to be renewed every year. The number of animals, it is the rule, can under no circumstance be raised on a permit. This, however does not imply that the livestock has stopped growing. It has already been noticed that the number of cattle in the State has been registering positive growth at each livestock Census. In 1992 the total number of animals was put at 52,62,704. At the same time the grazing area is continuously shrinking. It becomes apparent from the data reproduced here below:

Year	Area closed to grazing for all animals throughout the year. (in sq. km)	per cent of	Total forest area (in sq. km)
1976-77	1920.80	9.18	20937.66
1977-78	2578.25	12.31 "	20942.53
1978-79	3489.33	16.77 "	20812.20
1984-85	5077.38	24.87 "	20423.29
1993-94	7019.60	20.36 "	34453.16

Source: Deptt. of Forest Farming & Conservation, H.P.—Annual Administration Reports.

No reliable data on actual number of buffaloes and other cattle of *Ban*-Gujars is forthcoming. It is evident from the select data tabulated below:

Division	No. of buffaloes permitted to graze	No. checked in dhars	No checked at check posts	Variation (3-2)
1	2	3	4	5
1972				
Dalhousie	2376	2660	2563	+284
Chamba	7378	11485	6955	+4107
Total	9754	14145	9518	+4391 (in excess by 44%)
1974				
Dalhousie	2421	2699	-	+278
Chamba	7456	10372	-	+2916
Total	9877	13071	-	+3194 in excess by 32%

Strangely enough from similar data collected in 1992 there emerged a vastly different picture (see Table 6.2). 17,284 buffaloes permitted to graze throughout the State, on check, were found short at 14,367.

The variation is at a considerable large scale. There is no apparent reason for the wild swings in some Circles nor for the uncanny accuracy in most other Circles except for flawed checking mechanism. The huge difference in count can be attributed also to another principal cause. The Gujars like other graziers are master at deception. They practice it in order to beat the departmental regulatory control and to evade payment of tax as is the general wont of a common Indian tax payer. According to an estimate, which is not far off the mark, the *Ban*-Gujars' cattle, largely buffaloes, number as many as 50,000. Even this figure forms only a small part of the total grazing problem[15], which, needless to emphasise, cannot be solved even if the buffalo population of this tribe is completely eliminated: permanent settlement of Gujars can at best solve only a part of the problem. On the other hand the need of the hour appears to be to evolve

Table 6.2: Animals Permitted to Graze throughout the State and Found on Check

Forest Circle	Animals allowed grazing					Found on check					Variation
	Buff.	Cow.	Horse	Calf	Total	Buff.	Cow	Horse	Calf	Total	Total Variation
Wild Life	2803	165	163	547	3668	2930	148	224	654	3956	+288
Nahan	218	38	-	-	256	218	38	-	-	256	-
Rampur	350	75	160	257	842	350	75	160	257	842	-
Shimla	1120	82	93	592	1887	1120	82	93	592	1887	-
Dharmsala	37	-	25	15	77	37	-	28	16	81	+4
Mandi	2167	133	116	1	2417	2167	133	116	1	2417	-
Kullu	893	17	367	1206	2483	893	17	367	1206	2483	-
Chamba	9696	1070	939	2211	13916	7152	717	780	1723	10372	-3544
Total	17284	1570	1863	4829	25541	14367	1210	1768	4449	22294	-3252

a new approach in the formulation of policy frame-work, which *interalia*, shall lay emphasis on:

(i) reduction of higher cattle land ratio; to increase productivity of pasture lands through substitution with improved lots;

(ii) plantation of fodder trees in the pastures;

(iii) strict regulation of nomadic grazing and assignment of grazing by Gujars to an independent agency;

(iv) regulated closure of forests from grazing & lopping;

(v) introduction of improved exotic breeds;

(vi) reduction of the herd size; and

(vii) promotion of stall feeding habit and cattle development through appropriate key village schemes.

Ecological Interaction

According to Dr. P.N. Khosla, Vice-Chancellor of Himachal Pradesh *Krishi Mahavidyalaya*, Palampur, 'grazing of cattle in the forests should never have been allowed in the first place. Permitting it without charging any fees amounted to giving the villager owning cattle a free hand to go on raising as many cattle as he could' possibly manage. On similar lines is the expert advide of Dr. J.A. Voelekar, an international expert. In the present-day Indian situation, he strongly feels 'the forests must be closed to grazing'. Recently a forest scientist participating in a seminar equated grazing by animals like goats in the forests to virtual 'committing ecological *harakiri*':

Heated debate over the extent of environmental consequences of grazing is on for quite some years now but for lack of in-depth studies and proper research, a pall of uncertainty hangs over it. Whatever sketchy and limited evidence is available at present reports a definite decline in diversity and regeneration of forests and grass lands. Soil erosion on an extensive scale is visible throughout the State. The forestors ascirbe the damage principally to over-grazing by livestock, both domestic and migratory. Gujars have been roundly blamed for the environmental degradation of the hills notwithstanding that there is no empirical evidence or scientific information to this effect. The most threatened and mostly believed destructive interaction of Gujars with nature is wild life. The Gujars are criticised for destroying their normal habitat particularly at high mountain ranges. The pheasants which are one of the most endangered species are fast dwindling in Chamba area mainly due to grazing by them. Incidence of illegal hunting is reported to be on the rise. It is alleged that guns provided for self-protection the Gujars use for illicit hunting. They are also blamed for heavy deforestation as they are reported to be cutting trees more than they actually require for their *kothas*. Indiscriminate lopping by them ultimately results in the withering of green trees. And for it too *Ban*-Gujars are held responsible.

The situation is grim and the first step that needs to be taken is the conduct of research in order to ascertain the extent of environmental degradation and to determine the carrying capacity of the pasture lands. It is only then that some efficacious working solutions would emerge for implementation by the State Government.

Notes and References

1. Frederick Bath, *Nomads of South Persia*; London, 1961.
2. H.P. Govt. Directorate *of Economics & Statistics, A Socio-Economic Study of Gujars*; Shimla, 1983. Also see Appendix-I.
3. H.P. Govt.Forest Deptt., *Report on the Grazing Problems & Policy of Himachal Pradesh* by B.S. Parmar; Shimla, 1959.
4. Jistu, D.C., A Study of Gujars—A Nomadic Tribe in Mahasu District, Himachal Pradesh; 1962 (unpublished).
5. "   "
6. H.P. Govt.Directorate of Economics & Statistics. *A Socio-Economic Study of Gujjars*; op. cit.
7. H.P. University-Institute of Tribal Studies. Social Transformation of Gujjar Tribe of Himachal Pradesh—*Tribal Development: Approvisal & Alternatives*; New Delhi, 1998.
8. H.P. Govt., Institute of Public Administration. *A Study on Different Aspects of Minorities in Himachal Pradesh with Special Reference to Gujars;* Shimla, 1994.

According to this Study nomadic Gujars are by and large landless, though a few here and there have acquired small plots of land not so much as to switch over to Agriculture but principally to earn a title to local grazing, which right incidentally is an adjunct of land ownership. Even those of them who have permanently settled and taken to farming as main occupation possess unviable plots of land-50 per cent between 1 to 5 bighas; 30 per cent 6-10 bighas and only 20 per cent more than 10 bighas of land, with no family generating from it annual income exceeding Rs.11,000.

9. Handa, O.C., *Textiles, Costumes and Ornaments of the Western Himalaya*; New Delhi, 1998.

10. Parmar, B.S., *Report on the Grazing Problem and Policy of Himachal Pradesh; Shimla*. 1959. op. cit.

11. H.P. Govt., Letter No. 22-11/71-5F dated 20.6.1972 read with No. 3-51/71-GAC dt. 14.6.1972.

    It was decided in the 6th meeting of Gujjar Welfare Board, held on 15-3-96 that for unauthorised grazing a penal charge of Rs. 16 be levied on per head of buffalo.

12. See recommendation 6 contained in paragraph 32 of the Committee's Report (1970). The Committee had recommended imposition of uniform rate of fee throughout the State for all species of livestock.

13. A high-level Grazing Advisory Committee was constituted to review the entire grazing policy of the Pradesh *vide* H.P. Govt. Notification No. Ft. 784-13/66 (M) dated the 29th February, 1968.

14. Negi T.S., *Scheduled Tribes of Himachal Pradesh: A Profile*: Meerut, 1976.

15. According to H.P. Department of Farming and Conservation for the year 1994-95, "as many as 627,510 animals have been reported to have grazed in State forests on permit at full rates.... Besides about 22-25 lakh animals are estimated to have grazed in the forests by right-holders...."

7

Economic Profile

"(A)lthough none of them have large fortunes like the merchants and bankers of the plains, yet the riches are much more equally divided, and the poorest people are never in want, for if even the grain be scarce, as it often is, yet their large flocks furnish an inexhaustible store."

Alexander Gerard in *Account of Koonawur in the Himalaya.*

Gerard was speaking of Kanuaras, the migratory graziers of Kinnaur and not of nomadic Gujars, who unlike them and the Gaddis of Chamba exclusively practise livestock rearing for subsistence. They possess neither a permanent home nor cultivated land as do the Gaddis and Kanauras, the two most populous pastoralists in the State. They are. overly well-to-do. Not so the Gujars, the poor cousins. The sheep and goats lamb and kid every year: the Gujar buffaloes do not calve as frequently nor profusely. Sheep are maintained largely for their wool. Of goats the financial value lies in their meat: upto 40 per cent in each flock are sold every winter. Profits from grazing make a dramatic difference to their income. The shepherd households in Bormann's survey[1] earn an average of Rs. 597 from agriculture and ten times more (Rs. 5,240) from herding. On the contrary it is solely from the wandering herds of buffaloes that the Muhammadan Gujars or the *Ban*-Gujars obtain their livelihood. This primarily involves the sale of milk, butter and clarified butter or ghi. Their extensive migratory movements take them to fairly remote areas. In these some-what inaccessible places, ghi is the form in which milk produce can be stored without spoiling. Manifestly ghi and milk are not as valuable as wool and mutton are. No other part or product of buffalo yields to him additional income worth the name. They have practically no other source to supplement income from dairy farming.

In this background it is rather hard to digest what Parmar has observed in his report (1959)[2] and which Negi has reproduced[3] as the 'officially expressed' view of *Ban*-Gujars' economic condition.

> The economic condition of the Gujar cannot be judged by their appearance or ornaments. The sight of a family of Gujars, moving up or down the hill, gives the impression that theirs must be a precarious existence and incredibly uncomfortable one. But it has got to be remembered that these are the only people who sell milk and ghee on a commercial scale. It is not possible to ascertain correctly as to how much profit a Gujar makes from the trade after paying the grazing dues, satisfying the requirements of petty officials and village dignitaries and getting the financial relief obtained by manuring private fields during transit. For all intents and purposes, it cannot be incompatible with his hard work particularly when the dues paid are low and grazing availed of enormous. My own impression is that, on the whole, they are better off than the *zamindars* with whom they live in symbiosis though some of them received a set-back during the disturbances of 1947 from which they have not wholly recovered.

In support of his conclusion, Parmar has not relied on any authentic economic indicators. Apparently what has swayed his judgement is the sole fact that 'the dues paid (by him) are low and grazing availed of enormous'. This factor may be a sound reason for raising the level of taxation, which actually he proposed, but cannot possibly form a true index of economic health of these people. The actual condition of their economy, is, what Negi succinctly described in 1976. Generally speaking the Gujar does not starve but the 'living that he ekes out of the nomadic economy forces him to lie at a very low level by modern standards.[4] Additionally, indebtedness, an important indicator of poverty, 'is almost ubiquitous' among them. The picture would be no different today. Devoid of any political clout and the noose tightening by ever-rising demand for reduction of his stock and growing limitation on accessibility to pasturage, his economic plight can better be imagined than described.

Sources of Income

Agriculture: Great majority of the Gujar families are land-less; though, in course of time, a few have acquired small plots; more, as pointed out earlier, to secure grazing rights than to change their hereditary pastoral occupation. According to an estimate (1983)[5] 88.17 per cent of them do not possess any landed property, not even a minuscule plot to raise a permanent structure to call their home. Of the remaining 12 per cent, around two-third, 7.10 per cent to be exact, own land measuring less than 4 acres; those possessing less than one acre each constitute half of them. Those who exceed this lowly average are few and far between. The holdings are far from fertile; for the most part these are stony and un-irrigated patches unable to yield much corn, growing mostly fodder and grass for the animals.

Their income from agriculture is negligible. 4.73% of seven per cent who had responded, it was less than Rs. 1,000; for 1.77% between Rs. 1,001-2,000; in respect of very few (0.59%) the income was above Rs. 2,001 but below Rs. 3,000. None was found to be earning income in excess of it. Even the picture of those of them, who are since settled and practice agriculture as the main occupation, is far from cheerful. Of the one hundred house-holds covered by the 1994 Study[6], it was found that 50% had less than 5 bighas of land; 29% between 6 to 10 bighas and only 20% possessed more than 11 bighas. From it, more than half, to be precise, 57% could raise annual income of less than Rs. 11,000; 13% between 11,001 and 15,000; 11% fell between 15,001-20,000 range and only 19% generated income of more than Rs. 20,000 per annum. Thus for majority of them (70%) too the agriculture has not proven a viable proposition.

Dairy Farming: Animal husbandry is the mainstay of *Ban*-Gujars' livelihood, and buffaloes their chief asset. Most of the families keep other domesticated animals, like oxen, cows, goats and poultry as well but their number in proportion to buffaloes is minimal, and the object service and not profit. In 1962 Jistu[7] came up with the following result in regard to such animals kept by the families he studied in their alpine pastures:

	Percentage of families keeping				
	Horses	Oxen	Cows	Goats	Poultry
Upto 2 animals	45.9	41.6	18.5	4.6	13.8
Between 3-4 animals	13.8	9.2	1.5	4.6	3.1
between 5-6 animals	-	3.1	-	1.5	12.3
between 7-8 animals	3.1	-	-	3.1	-
between 9-10 animlas	-	-	-	3.1	-

Represented in another form it brings out that most of the households keeping cows had four or lesser number of them; poultry comprised less than 6 birds, goats less than 10 and horses between 2 to 4, with those keeping 7-8 horses being an odd exception. Obviously their small number could possibly yield no income.

As regards buffaloes he found that the sixty five families he had covered, had in all, 1,411 buffaloes, both milch and dry (including calves) on an average owning 21.7 animals per house-hold. Of the above only 347 were milch animals with ownership pattern as shown below:

No. of milching buffaloes	No. of families	Percentage to the total families
1-3	24	37.0
4-6	20	30.8
7-9	11	16.9
10-12	5	7.7
13-15	1	1.5
16-18	1	1.5
19-21	3	4.6

It is thus seen that large number, *i.e.,* 67.8 per cent owned 6 or less milching buffaloes and only 24.6% possessed more but not exceeding 12 cattle head. Those owning less than 6 milching buffaloes formed the vast multitude and it was only the 31 per cent segment which owned a larger number to enable the average to find its level at 5.3 milch buffalos per family. This result does not vary much from the conclusion of the 1983 Study covering the entire State. According to it an average family's holding of both milch and dry cattle comprised 8.23 buffaloes and 24.8% of the families, each having more than 10 animals, owned around 49% of the total number of buffaloes. Incidentally it approximates the average which the 1994 Study has revealed in respect of the resident Gujars. As per its results, an average Gujar family has 7 animals comprising of buffaloes and she-calves with 54% possessing between 1 to 5 followed by 29% in the range of 6-10 and only 20% having more than 20 cattle heads. That the Chamba Gujars, in particular, possess larger herds is brought out by another Study,[8] the subject of which, formed 40 Chamba migratory families and an equal number of settled families in the foothills of Dhauladhar. According to it on an average each family possessed 14 buffaloes; individual possession varying between 2 to 35.

How much milk does a Gujar buffalo yield was probed during 1983 in order to work out a nomadic Gujar's annual income form his herd. The result of this exercise showed that by and large the Gujar buffalo is poor milker, ill nourished and of poor breed, yielding on an average only three litres of milk per day or even less than that, by as much a large number as 17.57% of the herd. Buffaloes yielding 2 to 3 litres milk were too numerous: to account for three-fourth of the entire milch cattle, with only one quarter giving 4-5 litres. Those exceeding this manifestly poor yield were a rare sight, one in ten.

Qty of milk	Percentage
2 litres	17.57
3 "	56.22
4 "	12.09
5 "	10.27
6 "	1.81
7 "	0.60
8 "	0.60
9-10 "	0.84

Average yield per buffalo 3.23 litres.

The milk yield per animal was however found higher in case of sedentary dairies than the migratory house-holds.[9]

To top it, the lactation period is too brief. It has been observed to last 6-7 months only (in 64.9% cases); exceeding by one or two months only in 25 per cent of the cases.

Lactation period	Percentage
4 months	4.14
5 "	7.10
6 "	57.39
7 "	7.10
8 "	23.09
9 "	1.18

Average lactation period ...6.7 months.

Winters are harsh on the animals: green forage is conspicuously missing; fodder is scarce and the Gujars are too poor to spend hard cash on the purchase of nutritious feed or oil cakes and grains, etc. The result is still lower milk yield during the months of October to April. Moreover the quality of milk of nomadic farms is poor compared to settled dairy farms, mainly due to the poor quality of fodder and undernourishment.[10]

During summer the *deras* graze the cattle in alpine pastures, which most of the time, are far removed from urban centres of population. Easy marketing not feasible, the Gujars have no option but to convert the milk into ghi. That explains why only 35% of the families are estimated to sell milk during summer. In winter when they are in the plains and it is convenient to find ready markets, the position reverses and majority (80%) take to selling of fresh milk rather than to go in for time-consuming and labour-intensive process of making ghi or *khoya*. Either way, as they say, the income is almost on the same scale.

According to the 1983 Study, income from milk and milk products was estimated between Rs. 1,000-3,000 in the case of 4.37% of the subject families; between 1,500-3,000 of 9.47%; Rs. 3,000-6,000 of 37.86%; Rs. 6,000-10,000 of 35.50% and between Rs. 10,001-15,000 of 11.83% of them. Only 0.97% families were found to be earning between Rs. 15,000-20,000 with none exceeding the latter figure. The average annual sale proceeds of dairy products by a *Ban*-Gujar family was thus estimated to be Rs. 6,392.82.

The resident Gujars, in contrast, derived comparatively less income from this source. The 1994 Study has shown that only 3% households were generating income of more than Rs. 10,000 per annum. To be precise, as many as 26% of them fell within the income range of Rs. 501-2,000; 37% between Rs. 2,001-5,001; 37% between Rs. 5,001-10,000 with the rest of the respondents (4%) making no gain at all, although they kept some livestock.

By and large *Ban*-Gujars are poor. Ready cash is scarce and very often they are obliged to borrow money. Village shopkeepers and *halwais*, to whom they sell milk and ghi every summer therefore are the most likely persons to be approached for small loans or advances. On their part these petty traders are generally not averse to making short-term advances; for the arrangement assures them a reliable source of supply of milk and ghi. Besides charging usurious interest they generally pay them much less for their produce, often half of what be the market price. This vicious practice, Gujars have since come to realise, is clearly detrimental to their interests. It was the verdict of 40% of the families contacted during 1983. More than half (55.6%) expressed preference for sale of milk at government collection centres. The main reason cited was the comparatively low price they were paid by the *halwais*. Though not happy with the milk pricing formula of the Dairy Development Corporation which they consistently have been pressing for upward revision of, the Gujars still appear in favour of sale at collection centres. Manifestly their demand for opening of additional collection centres located nearer their camps/residences is reflective of it. So large do they consider their contribution to the success of the State's milk supply schemes that they have felt justified in claiming representation on the Board of Management of the State Dairy Corporation.

Expenditure

Annual expenditure of a Gujar family may be classified under three main heads, namely, *(a)* self-maintenance, *(b)* maintenance of cattle and *(c)* expenditure incurred on migration and to satisfy sundry claims on family's purse.

Of the gross receipts of Rs. 6,392.82 from the animal husbandry (1983) it was estimated that an amount of Rs. 2,054.62 was spent by a *Ban*-Gujar on the purchase of fodder—18.35% families spending more than Rs.3,000 per annum; 15.38% between Rs. 2 to 3 thousand, and the rest constituting a big majority of 66% spending less than Rs. 2,000 in an year. The consumption expenditure on other essential house-hold items was estimated at Rs. 3,327.44. Broken up it accounted for:

(i) Cereals	... 47.47%	*(ii)* Sugar/gur	... 10.91%
(iii) Vegetables	... 4.50%	*(iv)* Pulses	... 3.89%
(v) Spices	... 2.95%	*(vi)* Tea leaves, etc.	... 2.45%
(vii) Kerosene oil	... 3.37%	*(viii)* Clothing	... 7.56%
(ix) Medicines	... 3.43%	*(x)* Festivals	... 4.51%
(xi) Miscellanous	... 8.96%		

In short, around 65% of the total expenditure was accounted for by rations, *viz.*, cereals, pulses, sugar, gur, tea leaves, etc. Another significant head of expenditure related to clothes and festivals (12%). The other side of the picture showed that around 60% of the families spent around Rs. 1,500-1,800 on food and 30% a bit more, i.e., Rs. 2,000-2,500. There were only 10% of them who incurred a little more on this account. Expenditure on clothing too reflected almost the same pattern of spending: 70% of the house-holds spending less than Rs. 1,000 and 30% around Rs. 1,200-1,500. Expenses on account of cost of medicines averaged Rs. 114/29; Rs. 90/99 on payment of grazing fees and taxes and Rs. 149/55 on celebration of various feasts and festivals.

Migration too makes a sizeable dent on a Gujar family's income. About one half of the families were found spending a shade less than Rs. 1,000 and 33% upto Rs. 1,500. The rest of the house-holds reportedly incurred some-what more expenditure on this score.

From the above it can safely be concluded that much of what they earn (70 to 75%), they have to spend on their own up-keep consisting of sparse food and poor and rough wearing apparel-hand to mouth living indeed. With whatever little is left over (25% of income), they have to make do for the care and maintenance of their herds of buffaloes, their only or chief source of income, as also to meet other sundry expenses including on migration.

An analysis[11] has shown that the quantum of expenditure increases during the winter months when fodder, oil-cakes and concentrates have of necessity to be purchased for the cattle; whereas during summer months expenditure on fodder is almost next to nothing. In winter increase is also registered on account of cost of fuel and foodgrains. In summer consumption of flour comes down because there is sufficient quantity of whey to supplement the diet. The increase, in winter it was found, went up by about 40% both on account of self maintenance and on cattle.

About resident Gujars it is revealed that on an average each house-hold incurred an expenditure of Rs. 5,486 on food and clothing. It was less than Rs. 5,000 in the case of 56%; between Rs. 5,001-10,000 by 30% and between Rs. 10,001-15,000 by the remaining 14% of the families. Expenditure on fertilizers, seeds and other agricultural inputs averaged Rs. 519; on education Rs. 667; on marriages —of son Rs. 12,075; of daughter Rs. 5,333; of a relation Rs. 577; on religious ceremonies Rs. 622; births and deaths

Rs. 1,447 and on other accounts Rs. 697. Oviously their standard of living is better than that of *Ban*-Gujars.

Savings

From these estimates it was concluded that on an average a *Ban*-Gujar family would make an yearly saving of Rs. 987.76, as shown below:-

Gross annual receipts	Rs. 6369.82
(-) expenditure on fodder	2054.62
Net average annual income from dairy farming of a *Ban*-Gujar family	4315.20
(-) consumption expenditure	3327.44
Net annual saving	987.76

Undeniably the above statistics are misleading and do not present the real or true picture of the economic well-being of the tribe. It is important to keep in mind numerous invisible items on which a family invariably has to incur some expenses. For example palm of various forest officials has to be greased in order to procure permits for pastures, manage to keep on the sly cattle more than allowed by the permit, and to graze in pastures not officially permitted. Sometimes for the user of village *shamlat*, local dignitaries have to be bribed. Again births, marriages and deaths in the family are normal occurrences which place unexpected strain on the family purse. Mortality of cattle is yet another cause of heavy financial drain. In the circumstances it would not be far from truth that none but only a lucky family would be able to save something for the rainy day.

The position of resident Gujars, on the other hand, is definitely better. They have income from service sector as well, which avenue, unfortunately, is denied to those roaming from place to place. The 1994 Study came to the conclusion that 60% of the house-holds were earning more than Rs. 20,000 annually from this source alone. 20 per cent of the families were reported to be earning between Rs. 15,001-20,000 with equal number of families making less than Rs. 15,000. In the backdrop of this highly remunerative source it is reasonable to agree with the finding that 76% of the families made annual saving upto Rs. 5,000;

9% between Rs. 15,001-20,000; 12% between Rs. 5,001-15,000 and 3% more than Rs. 20,000 per annum.

Whatever little they save, *Ban*-Gujars do not put in a bank. They would rather convert it into jewellery for their women-folk, purchase a buffalo or acquire a small piece of land, or else lend a part of it to some needy kinsman. It is only the resident segment, which has come to make use of the banking institutions. According to the 1994 Study referred to supra, even among the permanently settled Gujars, only 48% were reported maintainting accounts with banks.

Indebtedness

Indebtedness among them is ubiquitous as Negi once remarked. The problem is endemic and is found in virulent form especially among the nomadic Gujars. Jistu found 80 per cent of them under debt though the amounts of loan do not by present-day standards seem excessive: 33.9 per cent families had borrowed less than Rs. 600; 23.1% between Rs. 600-1,200; 9.2% between Rs. 1,200-1,499 and only 13.8% in excess of Rs. 1,500. With the passage of time burden in terms of amount of principal no doubt has considerably gone up. It is proven from the data reproduced in the 1994 Study, although it relates exclusively to the settled Muslim Gujars. According to it, 68% of the households had borrowed money amounting less than Rs. 5,000; 27% between Rs. 5,001-10,000 and 5% even more than that amount. Another interesting peculiarity Jistu came across was that in all the instancs the loans were short-term advanes mostly cleared on year to year basis. What they borrow in lean winter months, they repay from what they earn during summer season. A few cases, though rare, where individual Gujars had to resort to distress sale of cattle in order to clear the debt also came to his notice.

Credit Facility

At the root of this phenomenon lies the *Ban*-Gujars' migratory form of life. With no permanent place of residence and no valuable assets to pledge, the small time money lenders instinctively exercise extreme caution when advancing loans to them, and so do the financial institutions. This finds corroboration in the official Study of 1983. It makes the point that 'the Gujars cannot get loans from the financial institutions because of two main handicaps, *viz.*, *(i)* most of them have no permanent place of settlement; and *(ii)* since their wealth consists mostly of cattle, they lack assets which can be pledged as security...'

As noted above their source of raising loans is neither a bank nor a co-operative society. One reason behind it is that majority of them donot know how to approach a bank. Again the procedure is so cumbersome and complicated that it takes a lot of time and they feel daunted additionally by the unhelpful or indifferent attitude of the functionaries. And finally and most importantly they possess no immovable property like land or house and so are unable to furnish a guarantee, to give surety or mortgage any valuable asset, an essential requirement to secure a loan or advance.

Loans however they must raise for marriage in the family: the evil of bride price is the bane of the tribe. 21.1% of the families in Jistu's study had raised loans on this single account and only 14% to acquire assets like cattle or land. The over-powering need, however, is of consumption loans to meet day-to-day domestic requirements of the men as also the beasts. This pressing need alone accounted for indebtedness in more than 50% of the subject families. This conclusion is not far off the mark what the later study of 1983 revealed. According to it 25% of the households had raised loans for purchase of consumer goods; 16.8% for buying cattle, etc. and 16.8% of them for other purposes including to meet expenditure on marriage, death and the like.

To float loans is not easy for *Ban*-Gujars. No bank or any financial institution would extend credit to them. 'Not even a single house-hold mentioned of having borrowed money from banks or other financial institutions in the organized sector,' observes the 1983 Study conducted under the aegis of the Himachal Government. Even indigenous bankers are chary to place complete trust in them. Because of some black sheep, who might have given a slip to his creditor, the whole tribe has come under cloud. Most of them (77%) therefore raise loans from petty shopkeepers, who supply their daily requirements of rations and animal feed on credit. The 1983 Study, however, revealed a much lesser percentage of households who borrowed money from the local money lenders. It placed this figure at 41.6% only. The rate of interest the money-lenders charge is killingly high. As much as 65.4% of the families Jistu studied, were bound down to repay in kind (ghi and milk) with another 7% making good the balance in cash. Those of them who raise loans from their wealthy kinsmen, however, pay back in cash only. Manifestly lack of easy credit facility keeps the *Ban*-Gujars encaged in debt trap and stonewalls any improvement in their economic well-being.

General Standard of Living

The life style of *Ban*-Gujars is chiefly pastoral in character, herding and migrating with their cattle from pasture to pasture the normal feature. Their chief wealth consists of buffaloes and the few other domestic animals they usually keep. As seen earlier an average family normally does not own more than 10-15 heads of cattle. As asset, the stock is not of much consequence; of poor breed with low milk yield, their buffaloes have poor market value. Majority of them are land-less. Those few (12%) fortunate to own it have very small holdings of one to four acres in area fit to be used as grass land. Tiny plots which some of them plough yield neither much grain nor any cash crop. Their other material stock consists of limited number of cooking utensils mostly made of cheap aluminum and hence of not much value. An outsider, however, would be attracted by their women laden with ornaments. These are mostly made of silver of doubtful purity. In 1962 Jistu estimated roughly that more than one half of the families possessed ornamental stock of a value below Rs. 200. Little more than one-third of them owned ornaments of the value of Rs. 400. Only 10 per cent of them, he found, claimed value of their this asset in excess of Rs. 500. Jistu had based his calculations valuing silver at Rs. 1/50 per *tola*. In the present day context their worth would still fail to impress any likely creditor.

Housing and living conditions constitutes an important indicator of economic well-being of a people. About nomadic Gujars the less said the better. After fifty-one years of Independence they are not a pretty sight. 88 per cent of them own no land nor have a roof over their head which they could call their home. To the tenements called *kothas*, which they construct or re-build year after year in the wilderness of far-flung pastures, they cannot claim any proprietary right. Their rough-built abodes with not more than solitary dingy living rooms, lacking in ventilation, are without running water or a light to dispel bleakness of cold and dreary nights. Surroundings are unhygienic what with the cattle tethered under the same roof and the dung heaped nearby in the open. Living on a poor diet of maize bread, gulped down with a little watery *dal* or *lassi*, morning and evening, all the year round, they present a pathetic picture of subsistence. All-pervading indebtedness and the money-lenders' usurious contracts fills their cup of misery. Illiteracy and ill-health, the twin evils signifying highest degree of backwardness, flourish merrily. Buffetted from all sides, married to poverty, the tribe virtually forms the most neglected, grossly disadvantaged and highly exploited section of society.

One of the main reasons of their economic backwardness is illiteracy. Literacy percentage amongst all the scheduled tribes of the State is low at 47.09% and amongst Gujars as a whole illiteracy is highest at 81.15% Nomadic Gujars are the most backward with illiteracy percentage in them ruling at 94%. Among them only 5.33% are primary and another 0.67% middle pass.[12] The main reason behind the abnormally high rate of illiteracy is that most of the time they are on the move in search of pastures. Their migratory and unsettled life is thus the greatest hindrance. It has also been seen that even where schools be within reach of their *deras,* they would not show much inclination to send their wards there. Maybe they need the services of children at home. And it is also possible that the advantage of giving education to their wards has not yet fully dawned on them.

References

1. Borman, Hans Harbert, *Shepherding in Dhaula Dhar* (Indo-German Development Project) Palampur, 1980.

2. Parmar, B.S., *Report on the Grazing Problem and Policy of Himachal Pradesh*; Shimla, 1959.

3. Negi, T.S., *Scheduled Tribes of Himachal Pradesh: A Profile*; Meerut, 1976.

4. Negi, T.S., *Scheduled Tribes of Himachal Pradesh: A Profile;* op. cit.

5. Himachal Pradesh Govt. Directorate of Economics & Statistics. *A Socio-economic Study of Gujjars:*Shimla, 1983. (Referred to as 1983 Report).

6. Himachal Pradesh Govt.—Institute of Public Administration. *A Study of Different Aspects of Minorities in Himachal Pradesh with Special Reference to Gujjars*; Shimla, 1994. (Referred to as 1994 Study).

7. Jistu D.C. (Delhi School of Social Work, Delhi University). *A Study of Gujjars—A Nomadic Tribe in Mahasu District, Himachal Pradesh*; Delhi, 1962. (Unpublished Project report).

8. Chauhan S.K. (H.P. Agriculture University, Palampur). *Credit Requirement in Dairy Enterprise—A Financial Study of Gujjars in Kangra District of Himachal Pradesh*: Palampur 1982. (Agricultural Economics thesis-unpublished).

9. Chauhan, S.K., -do-

10. Chauhan, S.K., -do-

11. Jistu, D.C., *A Study of Gujjar—A Nomadic Tribe in Mahasu District,* op cit.

12. Singh Gopal and Manohar Kamal. Social Transformation of Gujjar Tribe of Himachal Pradesh—*Tribal Development; Appraisal Alternative*; (Ed.- S.K. Gupta, V.P. Sharma and N.C. Sharda); New Delhi, 1998.

8

Socio-economic Development:
Appraisal and Alternatives

Tribals—Autoehonous People

The so-called 'tribals' are the indigenous autoehonous people in the sense that they had been long settled in different parts of the country before the Aryan-speaking peoples penetrated India to settle down first in the Kabul and Indus valley and then over a period spanning a millennium and a half to spread out over large parts of the country mainly along the plains and the river valleys. At a much later stage of history, there came to this land other civilized foreigners, in small numbers, like the Greeks, the Partheans and the Romans besides nomadic-pastoral tribes, in wave after wave, from the steppes of Central Asia, beginning with the Sakas and ending with the Turks and Mongols.

There is enough linguistic and archaeological evidence to suggest that the pre-Aryan indigenous people were settled originally in the fertile plains and the river valleys of the country. Under the mounting pressure of superior social organization with a superior techno-economy of Indo-Aryans, these so-called tribals were slowly but surely obliged to yield bit by bit to farther and farther areas until they came to find refuge in the relatively more inaccessible regions covered with dense forests, hills and large mountain slopes. This tight squeeze went on for centuries, moving slowly and steadily but in a very relentless manner till it came to a halt in very recent times. The cumulative and ever-increasing pressure of the superior economic, political, social and cultural forces was not easy to resist by the less-favoured tribes. More or equally superior peoples, like the Greeks, the Romans and a few others, who had come in small numbers, were not much affected by similar pressure; for they seem to have found it convenient for some reason or other, to merge themselves in the vast ocean of Indian humanity. By far the largest number of foreigners, who had entered, in wave after wave, were the Central Asian nomadic and pastoral-nomadic people. Once they were in India for two or three generations, majority of them, gave up their traditional nomadic-pastoral way of life in favour of dominant agriculture economy. But some large and small groups of them did not adopt agriculture as their primary vocation and preferred to retain the pastoral-nomadic habits of life. Why did they make this choice is not of much concern here. The fact is the remnants of them, who did not integrate in the main stream over the time, are still found in considerable number in Kashmir, Himachal Pradesh, Uttar Pradesh, Haryana and even in Maharashtra. Ban-Gujars, the nomads of Himachal Pradesh belong to that race. Though not scheduled as a tribe till 1956, they constitute a most significant category of pastoral class. Their backwardness is all pervasive judged by an exceptionally high level of illiteracy and their unhealthy living conditions. In relative security, seclusion and isolation they have been living for centuries in varying levels and degrees of contact and communication with the non-tribal people of the State. But whatever the degree or stage of contact and inter-relationship, they have on the whole, succeeded in maintaining their separate identity and their own socio-religious and cultural life.

Assimilation

Independence, democracy and adult franchise have released many social forces on the Indian scene. These currents are seen in play in many areas of our social, political, economic and cultural life. Some of these forces are creating ripples in this community as well. Basically it is a search for identity; for a sense of belonging and for self-determination of their place in the emerging social order. Their old order is fast disintegrating. The basic problem now is to draw and assimilate them into the national mainstream. The task is as much ours as theirs. A realisation is dawning on them that it is no longer possible nor good for them to remain aloof and continue on the old path in a futile attempt to find a place under the sun outside the national mosaic. They believe that a niche of their own they have to seek within the Indian society, of course, consistent with their concept of honour. It is time their competence is developed to enable them to face the competition of a developing society and to meet the challenges of an uncertain future. Harmonization of the wider national and their self-centered tribal interests is presently the key issue, which the administrators, planners, the anthropologists and the social scientists, all have to pool their intellectual resources, insight and experience to suggest how best to attend.

Scheduling of Gujar Tribe

The British Government in India introduced the classification of 'tribe' to designate various people called 'indigenous', 'aboriginal', 'hill' and 'jungle tribes'. The word 'tribe' had been hitherto used by European historians to refer to such distinctive group of people as the Gauls or the Anglo-Saxons in Europe and such autonomous political groups as Lichchivi, Mulla, Yaudheya and Khasha in ancient India, or such wide descent groups as the tribes of Israel or the Arab tribes in Western Asia. Social anthropologists like Rivers were using the word in reference to the people of Melanesia where each hill top or valley sheltered groups of people who were constantly at war with each other. In the Indian context efforts have been made to find common denominators of the word. The Commissioner for Scheduled castes and Scheduled tribes in his report for the year 1952 listed eight common features. Because they lived away from the civilised world in inaccessible parts lying in the forests and hills; spoke the same language; professed primitive religion known as 'animism' before they converted to Islam; followed traditional occupation; had nomadic habits and their techno-economic backwardness seem to be the considerations which weighed with the Kaka Kalelkar Commission. In this no mean part was played by Pt. Dharam Dev Shastri,[1] a pioneer social worker among the backward Gujars, Pangwals and Gaddis of Chamba. With his deep knowledge of their ways of life and intimate acquaintance with their socio-cultural and economic peculiarities, he was able to produce convincing evidence before the Commission when they visited Chamba. The Gujar conference (Chamba 1956) which was inaugurated by B.N. Datar, the then Minister of State for Home Affairs and which was attended among other dignitaries by L.M. Srikant, the Commissioner for Scheduled castes and Scheduled tribes, went a long way in strengthening their claim. Consequently in 1956, Gujars in Himachal Pradesh were notified Scheduled tribe. It is a pity that despite endorsement of the claim at subsequent Gujar conferences and exertion on the part of the Government of Punjab and later of Himachal Pradesh, area restriction has not been removed and the Gujar residents of the territories, which came over to Himachal Pradesh in 1966 as a sequel to the re-organization of the State of Punjab, remain deprived of the privileges, which the Constitution of India guarantees to the Scheduled tribes.

State's Tribal Policy

With the attainment of independence, it was realised by the national leaders like Mahatma Gandhi, Pandit Jawaharlal Nehru and Sardar Patel that in free India the tribals would have a fortune no different from the rest of the people. The Constituent Assembly debates[2] viewed in the backdrop of historical perspective best illustrate the emergence of State policy in relation to the tribes. The Sub-committee under the chairmanship of V.A. Thakkar constituted by the Constituent Assembly was pre-dominantly occupied by the humanitarian idiom of protecting the tribal economic interests and safe-guarding their way of life in order to ensure their development 'so that they might take their legitimate place in the general life of the country'. Bearing in mind the tribal simplicity, their weaknesses and their exploitation, the Sub-committee had recommended provision of statutory safe-guards covering among other matters, their economic upliftment and protection of their traditional customs and institutions. The proposals in essence contain the seminal ingredients of the State's Tribal policy. The policy in short is grounded on the basic premise that tribal advancement cannot take place in isolation and has to form an integral part of the development of the Indian people as a whole. Manifestly the policy speaks unambiguously in terms of assimilation of the tribals with the rest of the society. In other words the axis of tribal development is their ultimate integration in the stream of national life. The sum total of the policy, as aptly defined[3] by Dr. Verrier Elwyn, is to help the tribal people to grow according to their genius and anything to impose on their tradition is not the intention.

Permanent Settlement

It appears that Vinobaji was the first person personally to advise the Gujars to give up nomadic life and to settle down.[4] This view he put forth in his very brief speech at the Gujar *sammelan* held at village Draman (Chamba district) on the 14th October. 1959. Picking up the idea, the Conference lost no time in passing a resolution to that effect. Soon after, the view found iteration at the third Gujar conference held at Pathankot on November 20,[5] the same year. Dr. Rajendra Prasad, the President of India, in his inaugural speech laid emphasis on the permanent settlement of Gujars: nomadism he described a dark spot on the fair name of civilization. Shri Morarji Desai, the then Finance Minister, suggested establishment of colonies for them in the periphery of towns and cities, and hoped to see all the Gujars rehabilitated by the end of third Five Year Plan. The first step in this direction was taken by the Himachal Pradesh Government soon thereafter in 1961-62. A pilot project—a centrally sponsored scheme—was formulated at an estimated cost of Rs. 308,000 to raise a colony in Sirmur district near Dhaula Kuan at Naurangabad. The idea was to settle 23 nomadic Gujar families in that colony. The lay-out provided[6] 23 residential units each consisting of a single living room (13′ × 9′) besides separate latrine and bath room. A *pucca* cowshed (36′ × 20′) was to be shared by two families. Besides, provision was made for infrastructural facilities like drinking water supply scheme, electrification, link road, a primary school and a community hall. The work which started in the last year of the second Five Year Plan was completed by the fag end of the third Five Year Plan at a cost of Rs. 264,748.90. The colony is situated at a distance of about 2.5 kilometres from the main road and after initial teething troubles has only in recent years become a full fledged permanent settlement.

Allotment of units in the colony was made subject to certain conditions. One of them required the allottee families to give up summer grazing. To this effect each family was made to file an affidavit before possession of a house, cowshed and the plot of land could be given. Come next summer and one and all left for their traditional pastures, and the deserted colony was temporarily occupied by the Giri-Bata Project authorities. In the meanwhile through employment of coercive measures and cancellation of forest permits, all the families were made to return to the colony. This they did in 1965.[7] Subsequently some more families poured in from time to time. In all presently there are 31 families permanently settled at Naurangabad.

Initially a total area of 70 acres had been earmarked for the colony but subsequently at the repeated representations of the resident families thirty more acres of land was added. It was decided to be allotted at the scale of 5 acres of land to each settled family. The Gujars who came first and cleared the land came to grab more than those who came later with the result that presently some of them actually hold more than 5 acres while a few possess even less than half an acre. The Welfare department, however shows, on paper though, that each family has 8 bighas of land. No Gujar family incidentally has been conferred with any legal title to the land and the house it occupies.

The original idea was that the Gujars would put the allotted land to growing of fodder for their cattle so that they no longer had the urge or need to move around in search of pastures. In the absence of proper guidance and incentives they instead took to crop farming just like the local *zamindars*. As a consequence the settlers were not dissuaded from sending their herds to higher altitude pastures during summer when locally fodder becomes scarce. But when deprived of forest grazing permits, they had perforce to think of reducing their stock. With the passage of time the situation has arrived when most of them have almost given up buffalo breeding and rearing as their primary profession. They still keep a few animals but more as an activity supplemental to agriculture, which, as 1994 Study[8] shows has now become their main occupation. Admittedly the basic parameters of the concept have been defeated in that professional dairymen have been forced by circumstances to switch over to agriculture. One, however, cannot lose sight of the myriad advantages the settled life has brought for them in its wake.

To ensure regular and adequate supply of drinking water in the colony, a tubewell was got bored about a kilometre or so away, reportedly at a cost of around one lakh rupees. Its management and maintenance, strangely, was handed over to the community, which was expected to employ technical personnel to man it properly. After a short time, as was inevitable in such circumstances, it went out of order because of mishandling and neglect. Rather than have it repaired and learning a lesson from the past mistake, to handover its maintenance to some government agency, the officials on the contrary made the Gujars the scapegoat and allowed the matter to rest there. With taps gone dry the Gujar women once again started long haul, morning and evening, for water to slake the thirst of their children, husbands, elders, the infirm and the sick as also of the dumb animals. Is it any surprise that with such an indifferent attitude and unimaginative and wooden bureaucratic approach the experience was doomed to failure from the very beginning.

A brief mention here of a few other similar ventures would not be out of place. In 1966 a Gujar colony for five families was raised at Sahu in Chamba district. Out of planned five only three residential units were raised. With the colony a plot of land measuring not more than 12-15 bighas was attached. The families who moved in however soon abandoned it. The main cause of failure of the settlement plan was that the Gujars had neither land to grow fodder for their cattle nor were any alternate arrangements made to meet their fodder requirement. The buildings remained unoccupied till 1987 when eventually[9] an *ashram* for Gujar children was opened there.

It is seen from the annual report on the working of the Welfare Department (H.P. Administration) for the year 1957, that an amount of Rs. 10,200 was sanctioned for construction of houses (20) and cattle sheds (14) for families of Gujars in Chamba district. Resume of achievements of Second Five Year Plan issued by the Directorate of Economics and Statistics (H.P. Admn.) lists 'establishment of a colony for the rehabilitation of nomadic Gujars in village Bhagori of Chamba district' as one of the few programmes taken up for the welfare of Scheduled tribes. Under the heading 'Welfare of the Backward classes', a government publication titled 'Third Five Year Plan (1961-66), brought out by the Planning and Development Department, recounts:

> *(iv) Settlement of Gujars*—The proposal is to set up 15 colonies, each colony having 15 units of two rooms tenements including kitchen and verandah, etc. One community hall will also be provided to each colony. It is anticipated that by the end of Third Plan, nearly 1,125 persons (225 families) will be settled in these colonies.

Sad to say all these proved still-born projects and nothing concrete was done at the ground level to rehabilitate the rest of nomadic Gujars in colonies established around towns and cities with a view to provide them easy access to market profitably their produce of milk, butter and ghi as was the original intention. At no stage it was conceived that they should give up their centuries-old profession. Dr. Rajendra Prasad, Morarji Desai, Raja Bajrang Bahadur Singh, one and all had visualised[10] their future in better managed and scientifically developed animal husbandry.

Permanent settlement is the only possible solution of their salvation, and the issue has continued to agitate the mind of the State government. No one however talks any more of establishing colonies for them. At present the thinking seems to be to allot them some land in the hope that it would attract them to lead a settled life and give up forest grazing. For some years now an exercise has been going on to identify the landless nomadic Gujars and also to select some land which could be allotted to them. The search has revealed that in all there are 1,010[11] such families scattered over six districts of the State with none traced in the remaining districts of Lahul and Spiti, Kinnaur, Hamirpur, Bilaspur, Solan and Una. They are 736 in Chamba, 39 in Kangra, 91 in Sirmur, 69 in Kullu, 74 in Shimla and only one in Mandi district. It is reported that 499 Chamba families would prefer to settle in Jawali and Nurpur teshils of Kangra district. No effort however has been made to locate land for them in that district. Likewise for five families living in Kalatope area of Chamba no land has been identified. However for the remaining 232 families land measuring 2,579.16 bighas, in all, has been selected tentatively. It is forest land and has to be de-notified first. The matter is presently under the consideration of the Forest Department, which if agreeable to the transfer, is bound under the law to approach the Govternment of India. Same is the position in regard to allotment of land to the families in other districts save for the solitary family in Mandi district, to whom a plot of five bighas is reported to have been recommended for sanction by the competent revenue authority. Of Kangra Gujars, 21 families are willing to settle in Nurpur tehsil and another 18 in Indora tehsil. For them forest land totalling 105 bighas has been identified. For 91 families of Sirmur district and 69 of Kullu district plots of forest land respectively measuring 590.04 and 300 bighas have been picked up. In Shimla district there are in all 74 families. Of these, four of Chopal and 12 of Rampur sub-division would rather settle in Paonta and Ani (Kullu district). For the rest the Deputy Commissioner Shimla has located 290 bighas of forest land.

The process of de-notification of forest land is cumbersome, time-consuming and full of procedural technicalities and so is apt to take years to be decided either way. There is a distinct possibility of the whole exercise coming to naught with the refusal of the Government of India to permit change in land-use. Possibly scenting failure, presently the State government does not appear to be in any hurry to decide as to how much land has to be allotted to each family and what are to be the terms and conditions of its lease or transfer. There is also no initiative in the offing to settle a package of incentives like house-building grant/loan, monetary assistance to purchase stock of good breed and to subside assured supply of fodder and concentrates and the like matters.

Hoping against hope that the proposal would ultimately mature, sooner and later, what each family would get as its share would not be more that a pocket-sized plot on which a house for the family and a shed for the cattle would leave very little to scratch for subsistence. To expect a normal sized family of 5/6 members to eke out a living exclusively from the produce of such a tiny plot, around 3 bighas in area, would be the joke of the century. It would thus be not wrong to assume that no seriousness is manifest in the attitude of the Government in the early settlement of these nomads, inspite of continued heavy biotic pressure the buffaloes of Gujars are said to be responsible for, hampering in consequence, proper forest conservation and re-generation.

This much about the State government's plan. But what does the affected party think? Are they reconciled to the idea of giving up their traditional social mores and to settle down permanently, and if so, what minimum facilities they would expect the government to extend. The Socio-economic survey of Gujars (1983)[12] probed this aspect as well and the Study is most revealing. It showed that 66.27 per cent families responded positively to the idea of permanent settlement and only a minority of 14.79% exhibited reluctance. May be they were wary of uncertainties the future in an entirely strange environment held. It is also possible that before making up their mind they wanted to be apprised of the details of assistance the government would extend. Willingness of the majority to settle down is affirmed by 57.39% of the families showing agreement to surrender their existing grazing rights. It is a revelation of immense significance. Contrary to general assumption the grazing permit once considered the most valued possession has since lost its old-world charm. Majority would rather willingly surrender the privilege only if they are reasonably compensated.

How much time would they need to make the transition from pastoral grazing to sedentary dairy farming provides another positive signal. Of the 50% who had responded to this question, as many as 32.56% were found ready to quit within three months though 17.15% wished a grace period of three more months. The Study further found all united in one view. All of them expected the government to bear entire expenditure on their settlement including on the construction of the residential house and shed for the cattle. Considering their general poor economic condition it is small wonder they responded that way. On yet another point the opinion has been equally vehement. None wanted to give up dairy farming altogether, but desired to supplement it with some other activity: agriculture the sole preference. Again all of them wanted land to be allotted: 54.57% considered 3 to 5 acres as the minimum size of a holding they could subsist on. There were a few (17.89%) who wanted the holding size in the range of 5-7 acres and still a few others (21%) who seemed content with a smaller holding of 3 acres or so. Around three-fourth of the respondents wanted provision of modern living conveniences like electricity, running water, education, health-care, veterinary services and marketing facility. Realising that in the changed atmosphere they would need some additional avenue of income, more than 60% opted for wage earning opportunities at or near the place of settlement as well.

More than a decade has elapsed since the conduct of 1983 Survey. With the passage of time it appears the urge to settle down has grown stronger. A recent survey bears[13] this out. Of the 300 respondents contacted, 246 or 82% have preferred settled life. Having seen with their own eyes how far the settled members of their own community have gone ahead, economically and socially, they now need no persuasion or motivation. They have become fully aware of the vast horizon of myriad career opportunities, which has opened before the wards of the settled families. In contrast the ever-mounting hardships they almost daily face in their interface with the black sheep of the various government agencies and the local peasantry; the realisation how oppressively they had been exploited in the past and still are befooled by the local *halwais* and shopkeepers; the educational, health care services and of various modern facilities, they acknowledge, they are depriving themselves; all these and similar other considerations have since opened their eyes to the hellish misery of their nomadic life. That is why now all of them have come to believe that unless they settle down at one place they would not gain the fruit either of the planning process or what the Constitution grants. And what is more, they have come to realise that in the present state they are not likely to gain a political clout, which they recognise, is an essential concomitant to reap the advantages of democracy. Present is thus ripe time for the government to intervene, evolve appropriate schemes and implement them in right earnest. To be effective, it may be added as a footnote that these should be executed not through the usual bureaucratic agency but by persons who are driven with missionary zeal.

Here it would be in order to dilate and offer a few suggestions. To make their permanent settlement even and smooth, a basket of concessions needs to be offered to *Ban-Gujars*. To charm, it must be attractive in packaging as also in contents. For example the plot for house and cow-shed might be given *gratis*. For raising the structures, each family might be advanced capital, a smaller part as grant and the rest on loan basis. In any case the quantum of both the components should be adequate to meet the total cost of material like timber, roofing, cement, iron and the like. Moreover the rate of interest ought to be low and recovery spread over ten to fifteen years of time.

Generally speaking for a family of 5-6 adults a land holding of less than 10 bighas, unirrigated as it is likely to be, at least to begin with, would lack viability. The answer to transform the small holding into a viable unit would lie in assuring increased productivity by taking up vegetable and cash crop cultivation besides harvesting high-yielding varieties of corn and wheat for self-consumption. In certain areas horticulture could have unlimited possibilities. The land might either be leased out at concessional rental or nominal cost to be recovered in easy instalments. Liberal *taccavi* loans would have to be advanced for the purchase of draft animals, source of power and manure, besides better seeds, agricultural implements, chemical fertilizers, etc.

It would be naive to expect that Gujars would abruptly give up dairy farming. Their dependence on it would continue for so long as additional income generated from agricultural operations does not make them partially or fully independent of it. The service sector too would take some time to absorb some of the unemployed in its fold and to provide succour or rather supplemental income to the families. From that view, therefore, the Animal Husbandry department would have to come forward with some bold and imaginative initiatives. For instance it may offer free of cost a buffalo of good breed in exchange for 2-3 of their existing poor milkers. The idea would have the additional advantage of weeding out surplus poor stock presently forming undesirable burden on limited grazing resources. To ensure that the buffalo so supplied is taken good care of, the department might consider appointment of veterinary surgeons as contact officers charged to pay regular periodic visits in order to oversee the animal's upkeep, tender advice; provide guidance and needed treatment to all their animals. He would also have to ensure regular supply of recommended doses of concentrates, fodder and medicines, of course, on subsidized rates. In course of time comparatively better milk yield of a single stall-fed good buffalo is apt to induce each family to discard its old stock and replace it with fewer animals of good stock. Stall feeding too is likely to gain formal acceptance.

Twenty to thirty buffaloes is considered the minimum herd size of an economically viable enterprise. Co-operative societies could be formed to maintain herds of this size so that modern methods of farming could be employed to generate employment and wealth. To be successful in organisation, it would further be essential to make credit available at reasonable terms as also to provide dependable services and goods sector which could under-write the technology input.

The rehabilitation scheme should provide for the proper marketing of milk as also regular supply of fodder, etc. In this context milk cooperatives can go a long way in ensuring this as also for the procurement of cattle feed and green fodder. Above all the confidence gained from successful operation of these self-managed units is bound to prove highly effective in their integration with the mainstream of society.

But so long as this does not happen, the pastoral Gujars would have to be permitted to graze their cattle in nearby alpine pastures: for according to scientists stationery husbandry is not all that good as is commonly believed to be. Besides leaving the natural fodder resources of high altitude pastures unutilised, high density of animal pressure on the vegetation near settlements results in higher erosion frequency. Moreover due to the small farm operation size and structure the cattle kept stationery are not sufficiently nourished by the domestic fodder production.

Colonization is after all not a bad alternative. As already seen adequate land is not available for all the nomads in the districts in which they presently live. In 1983 a significant number of Gujars (63.63%) had expressed desire to settle in Punjab. The time is past now to pursue this line of action. A better idea would be to locate a few colonies of them around towns in the districts of Una, Hamirpur, Bilaspur, and Solan, etc., where presently no Gujars live. Incidentally these are the areas where tribal population is negligible. For instance the percentage of tribal to the total population is 0.06 in Hamirpur; 0.14 in Kangra; 0.01 in Una; 2.70 in Bilaspur; 0.64 in Solan; 1.61 in Sirmur; 0.71 in Shimla and 1.21 in Mandi district. There is vast scope to absorb youths of this tribe against reserved vacancies, which presently go abegging. Gujars are the best trackers in forests. Unemployed Gujar youth thus provides good material to be employed as guides in the National Parks or as forest guards or *rakhas*. As a measure of abundant caution it has to be ensured that the scheme that might be put on the anvil should not suffer from the shortcomings which came to light when colonies were established in the early sixties at Naurangabad and Sahu. Truly has it been said that man learns from his past mistake and only a fool insists on repeating it.

As already observed chronic indebtedness has been a major constraint in the economic development of Gujars. The solution lies in energetic tackling of this problem through organising a debt redemption machinery and setting up a revolving fund to pay off the amounts of debt. This end, if need be, could be achieved through the instrumentality of legislation. To ensure that the *Ban*-Gujars donot slip back into the clutches of money-lenders, suitable provision for non-productive consumption loans might have to be built into the system of cooperative thrift and credit societies.

Education, which widens one's perspective on life and society, is one area where much way has to be traversed. As mentioned earlier, the literacy percentage among *Ban*-Gujars is very very low, only around 5 per cent. Students of this community residing in Churah tehsil of Chamba district, for instance, have to travel 20 to 24 kilometres in order to reach a Middle school. The situation is no better else where. Whereever Gujars are settled, therefore, adequate provision of elementary and secondary institutions would have to be planned with facility made accessible within walkable distance. Thought would also have to be spared to devise measures to reduce the level of drop-out at different levels. For the nomadic Gujars emphasis should be laid on opening of sufficient number of *ashrams*. At least one such hostel at each of the six districts, where currently they are found, should be opened. In order to combat total illiteracy among the girls, separate hostels exclusively for the girls might be opened. Besides providing free board and lodging these hostels should be equipped with good functional libraries and teaching staff for extra coaching.

Gujar embroidery is unique in itself. This art needs to be preserved and developed amongst the girls. There is great possibility in it to making them self-sufficient economically.

Public awareness to different development programmes is at a very low ebb among the community. Unless the administration informs them of their potentiality and raises the level of awareness of how to avail the facilities which are offered, it would be futile to expect any good coming out of the vast planning endeavour.

These suggestions are illustrative only. Exhaustive planning naturally lies in the domain of experts.

Welfare and Development

A State committed to a policy of growth with social justice has necessarily to devise policies and programmes in a manner which minimizes varying clashing pressures, ensures that benefits from all sectors of development flow in equitable and just manner to all groups and communities and reduces socio-economic cleavages. The Constitution of India has declared in its Preamble that it aims at securing for all its citizens, 'Justice: social, economic and political; Liberty of thought, expression, belief, faith and worship; Equality of status and of opportunity, and to promote among them all, FRATERNITY assuring the dignity of the individual and the unity and integrity of the Nation.' In the Directive Principles of State Policy, it is enshrined that 'the State shall strive to promote the welfare of the people by securing and protecting as effectively as it may a social order in which Justice: social, economic and political shall inform all the institution of the national life'. Article 46 of the Constitution further postulates that 'the State shall promote with special care the educational and economic interests of the weaker sections of the people, and, in particular, of the Scheduled castes and the Scheduled tribes'. The goal set by the Constitution assures a progressive life to the members of the weaker sections of the community. The goal, in essence, is to emancipate them from all forms of exploitation.

In line with the constitutional postulate, late Pandit Jawaharlal Nehru, the first Prime Minister of independent India had advocated a policy of *panchsheel* for the betterment of the quality of life of the Indian tribes within an environment unpolluted by any outside influence or imposition of social standards alien to their nature and genius. In consonance with this policy Dhebar Commission and Shilu Ao Committee, both urged for the tribals' gradual socio-economic advance with the ultimate objective of integrating them with the rest of the society by bringing them at par with it within a reasonable period of time. However nothing tangible exclusively for the tribals was done till the Fourth Five year Plan. No appreciative study was conducted of their peculiar needs nor any specific strategy for their development was hammered out. It was only on the eve of the Fifth Five year Plan that the Tribal Sub-Plan strategy was evolved which continues to operate in shapes refined from time to time on the basis of experience gained in implementation.

In Himachal Pradesh main emphasis has been laid on the socio-economic development of the tribals rather than on the second prop of this policy, namely; protection against exploitation. This strategy seeks to develop human resources and infra-structure judiciously mixing it with beneficiary-oriented programmes. Before this new concept got under way in 1974-75 planned effort for the tribals at large formed an integral part of the sectoral development under different Five Year Plans. The allocation of funds for development of the tribes and the Tribal areas formed part of the general sectoral allocation with no separate assignments made exclusively for them. Lacking any direct thrust the programmes tended to be formulated in ad-hoc manner and lacked perspective. They were mostly in the nature of individual-oriented welfare programmes like housing subsidy, stipends to school-going children of primary and middle standard and a few scholarships to students aspiring to pursue higher studies. Likewise the State Plan allocations were made in the form of grants-in-aid and subsidies, again to select individuals.

A count may now be taken of the advantages which flowed from this approach to individual beneficiaries and the Gujar community at large. In the year 1956-57 following achievements find mention in the Annual Administration Report of Himachal Pradesh Administration for the year 1957:

    (a) an expenditure of Rs. 5,653 incurred on the appointment of a mobile teacher and on stipends paid to Gujar students.

(b)   an expenditure of Rs. 2,500 incurred to establish
a multi-purpose cooperative society with the object
to market milk and milk products of *Ban*-Gujars.

In addition, under the schemes sponsored by the Central
Government for the welfare of Gujars, another provision of
Rs. 11,140 was made for the mobile teaching staff; to grant
stipends and as aid for privately managed schools. Provision
was also made to open one mobile veterinary dispensary
and an amount of Rs. 560 was spent on the purchase of
some concentrates for buffaloes. Grant-in-aid, amounting
to Rs. 4,800 was sanctioned with a view to enable Gujars'
cooperative society to install a cream separating and ghi
making unit. An amount of Rs. 10,200 was disbursed as
house and cattle shed subsidy.

In the year 1958-59 schools at Jangi, Sillaghrat and Palur,
all the three in Chamba district, were started for Gujar
students. Apparently the peripatetic scheme had flopped
by this time. It is said, the mobile teacher did not receive
salary regularly nor could he adjust to the nomadic way of
life. After a long break spanning over more than forty years,
the old idea of mobile schools seems to have once again
caught the fancy of the administration. Opening of one such
school in Chamba district to move alongwith a group of
families which bond together for transhumance is the
instance in point. The same newsitem (*The Tribune,* June
23, 1998) which reported the launch of the project
incidentally highlighted the view point of the Gujars, who,
as per the report, feel 'that instead of starting mobile schools,
the government should open *bal-ashrmas* where their
children could stay permanently and receive education'; for
'it would be somewhat difficult for the entire school to keep
moving with them'.

To increase milk yield of buffaloes some new grasses were
introduced in six pastures of Church division (Chamba
district). Rupees ten thousand were spent and churning
machines purchased with this amount were distributed
among deserving Gujar families. For the construction and
repair of houses subsides totaling Rs. 25,000 were given to
a few families. In 1959-60 ninety more Gujars were like-

wise assisted to construct and repair houses and cow-sheds. In 1960-61, in addition to four continuing primary schools, one *Ashram* school was opened. These institutions continued to be maintained during 1961-62 and 1963-64. *Paravati Adimjati Sewak Sangh*, a voluntary organization working for the welfare of tribals including the Gujars was given grant-in-aid to continue its work. In all during the First and Second Five Year Plans an aggregate expenditure of Rs. 71,943 was incurred on the welfare of all scheduled tribes and backward classes. Out of an allocation of 99 lakhs for the Third Five Year Plan, an amount of Rs. 291,300 only was expended in 1964-65.[14] Apparently share of Gujars, as seen above, was ridiculously small, too small to make any dent in removing the general poverty and backwardness of the community.

This account would be incomplete without a brief description of the yoe-man service which the *Adimjati Sevak Sangh* Delhi rendered, in particular, among the most backward Gujars of Chamba area. Soon after it organized the first Tribal Conference in 1956, this voluntary organization launched an illiteracy eradication programme. That year they started two schools for Gujar boys and girls at a total cost of Rs. 3,247. At its initiative the Chamba district administration formulated an integrated programme, which again through its efforts, it got funded by the Central Government. The main areas of thrust of this programme were elementary education, housing subsidy, promotion of milk supply cooperative movement and to improve the breed of their stock. It is estimated that over the three years of its operation the Schemes cost an aggregate amount of one lakh and a couple of hundred rupees. In particular the scheme relating to grant of housing subsidy evoked positive response. Majority of Gujar families came forward and vied with each other to improve their living quarters. The initiative to improve poor breed of buffaloes, however, did not make much headway. Possibly faulty planning and slip-shod manner of implementation were responsible, in part at least, for its failure.

The Fifth Five Year Plan, regarded the water-shed in the history of tribal development, and all the subsequent Plans since have focused their undivided attention on the development of tribals inhabiting the tribal project areas and the Scheduled Areas. The entire gamut of planning has focussed exclusively on the welfare of the local tribals and the territories comprising the Integrated Tribal Development Projects of Kinnaur, Lahul, Spiti, Pangi and Bharmour.

Though the tribal areas comprise 42.49% of the State's total geographical area (respectively 23,655 and 55,673 sq. kms.) these are populated by only 2.93% of the total population of the State. For 151,433 persons, the Sub-Plan out-lay has peaked at 9% of the total State Plan out-lay. For example from 1991-92 to 1996-97 it has been of the order[15] of:

Year	State Plan (Rs.)	Tribal Sub-Plan (Rs.)
1991-92	4065000	365850
1992-93	4905000	437400
1993-94	5500000	497667
1994-95	6500000	585000
1995-96	7500000	675000
1996-97	9000000	810000

As *Ban*-Gujars donot populate these areas, obviously they figure nowhere in the scheme and out of the massive investment not a single penny has been spent to beat back their backwardness.

For tribals dispersed outside these areas Modified Area Development approach, a child of the Sixth Plan, concentrates on Chamba and Bhatiyat pockets. Though a sizable population of Gujars of Chamba is found in these areas, they are again the losers because of their nomadic way of life. The SCA supplementation under MADA, more over, has been at a negligible scale: Rs. 4.94 lakhs (1981-82) rising to Rs. 13 lakhs in 1994-95; Rs. 14 lakhs in 1995-96 and to Rs. 15 lakhs during 1996-97.

For the 37% of the total Scheduled tribe population dispersed outside these specific areas, the Union Welfare Ministry came out in 1986-87 with additional SCA supplementation. From a rupees 12 lakh budget in 1994-95 it has now risen to Rs.30 lakhs. How was it distributed[16] in 1996-97 may be seen from the following Table 8.1.

Tribal Sub-Plan 1996-97

Budgeted Outlays for Scheduled Tribes outside Tribal Areas (SCA)

(Rs. In lakh)

Sl No.	Major Head/ Head of Dev./ Scheme	Total	Ind.	Bilaspur	Chamba	Hamirpur	Kangra	Mandi	Kullu	Shimla	Sirmour	Solan	Una
1.	2.	3.	4.	5.	6.	7.	8.	9.	10.	11.	12.	13.	14.
	1. Horticulture:												
2401	Grant in aid to STs outside tribal area	15.00	-	2.01	5.60	0.05	0.21	2.35	1.83	0.92	1.50	0.50	0.03
	Total: Horticulture:	15.00	-	2.01	5.60	0.05	0.21	2.35	1.83	0.92	1.50	0.50	0.03
	2. Education:												
2202	1. Exp. On scholarship to ST girls (VI-VII) outside tribal areas.	9.00	9.00										
	2. Exp. On scholarship to ST girls (VI-VIII) outside tribal areas.	6.00	6.00										
	Total Education:	15.00	15.00										
	GRAND TOTAL	30.00	15.00	2.01	5.60	0.05	0.21	2.35	1.83	0.92	1.50	0.50	0.03

It does not require much mental exercise to conclude that of this very small cake the share of *Ban*-Gujars could not have been more than a few crumbs. The result is that the initiatives of the Central Government and the Himachal Pradesh Government spread over last fifty years have completely failed to make any impress on their socio-economic upliftment nor have these exerted any transformative •pressure on the *Ban*-Gujars' traditional social, political and economic structure.

Gujar Welfare Board

Equally ineffectual has been the institution of Gujar Welfare Board conceived with high hopes. For the very first time it was constituted in the year 1983. With Chief Minister its chairman it aroused a very high level of expectations amongst the nomads as also the social workers. It however failed to inspire much hope and confidence during its short life, which came to an end in December 1989. No one thereafter thought of its revival. After a lull lasting more than four years it was all of a sudden resurrected in 1994 when a new Board was notified (24.5.94). The incumbent Board has been reconstituted since 1st July, 1997. The Chief Minister continues to be its chairman and he is aided and advised by a motely crowd of 49 members of whom 29 are non-official nominated members, who are mostly Gujars, landless and nomadic though they donot look to be.

The Board has been meeting once or twice a year ever since its revival. So far it has held eight meetings to attend to the grievances of the community, mostly relating to particular localities or institutions. Achievements are neither significant nor many in number. Failures one can name many. For instance it has not exerted much to win recognition as Schedule tribe for its left-out community members hailing from the territories formerly of pre-1966 Punjab. Likewise it has not created any beneficial influence on policy formulation regarding their grazing rights. Failure to claim a larger share of Plan funds for Gujars has been its another dismal performance. It may appear harsh but the truth is that there is no important activity which the Board could justly claim its significant or remarkable achievement.

India celebrates fifty years of Independence. Was *Ban-*Gujars' heart in it? For them the search for home remains elusive with no ray of hope to lift their heart. Socially, politically and economically, Himachal Pradesh is on the cusp of great change but not the *Ban-*Gujars. There are myriad ways they are oppressed. Their pain and misery is fathomless. In the world of today verily these people are lagging behind every other weaker section of society. Their material decline has meant weakening of their social and psychological make-up undermining their personality and sense of well-being. By going deeper and deeper into their primeval reserves, they have become vulnerable to various unfamiliar and unnamed dangers. There is no doubt that a fairly rapid alienation from the tribal matrix is going on amongst them but the process is both subtle and slow. No doubt in appearance they have begun to adopt new premises for a different way of life but their harmonious integration with and happy assimilation in the mainstream is apt to take some time and more than time it calls for deep understanding of their psyche and tender handling of their feelings and sentiments.

Notes and References

1. Bhardwaj, A.N., *Tisri Gujar Tribal Conference, Pathankot* (Hindi); Salogra (Solan) 1960.

2. Parliament of India Secretariat, *Constituent Assembly Debate*, Vol. 3, (30-4-1947); New Delhi.

3. Verrier Elwyn, Dr., *A New Deal for Tribal India*; New Delhi, 1963.

4. Shashi, S.S., Dr., *The Nomads of Himalayas*; Delhi 1979.

5. Bhardwaj A.N., *Tisri Gujar Tribal Conference*, op. cit.

6. See Reply to unstarred question No. 30 answered on 20-7-1998 in Himachal Pradesh Vidhan Sabha.

7. Himachal Pradesh Govt.—Directorate of Economics & Statistics, *A Socio-economic Study of Gujjars*; Shimla, 1983.

8. Himachal Pradesh Govt.— Institute of Public Administration., *A Study on Different Aspects of Minorities with Special Reference to Gujjars*, Shimla, 1994.

Out of 100 Gujar households studied, including a few of Naurangabad, agriculture was found the main occupation of 73 percent and animal husbandry.of only 16 percent.

9. See Reply to unstarred question No. 30 of 20.7.1998. (op. cit)

10. Bhardwaj, A.N., *Tisri Gujar Tribal Conference,* op. cit.

11. See Reply to Unstarred Q No. 30 of 20.7.1998. (op. cit.)

12. Himachal Pradesh Govt.—Directorate of Economics & Statistics, *A Socio-economic Study of Gujjars*; Shimla, op.cit.

13. Himachal Pradesh University-Institute of Tribal Studies, *Tribal Development: Appraisal and Development*; New Delhi. 1998.

14. Himachal Pradesh Administration, *Annual Administration Report for the Year* 1964-65; Shimla, 1965.

15. Himachal Pradesh Govt.—Tribal Development Department, *Draft Annual Tribal Sub-Plan,* 1996-97; Shimla. 1996.

16. Himachal Pradesh Govt.—Tribal Development Department, *Annual Tribal Sub-Plan 1996-97—ITDP-wise Schematic Budgeted Outlays*; Shimla, 1996.

Appendices

Appendix I

Recommended routes, checking posts and control on movement in respect of nomadic Gujars' buffalo herds, as per Parmar's

Report on 'The Grazing Problems and Policy of Himachal Pradesh' Shimla, (1959)

Extracts

Grazing Policy for Chamba and Churah Forest Divisions

Chapter - VI

103. *Control of the movements of flocks and herds–*

(a) *Registration and enumerations*-It has been done in the case of Gujars only. It should also be done for the migratory and nomadic flocks of sheep and goats on the lines suggested before.

(b) *Routes fixed or not*-Routes are not fixed. Herds and flocks follow many routes on their summer and winter movements. Following routes are suggested to be fixed:

For Bhanier Gujars:

(i) Nurpur-Chamba road *via* Ghatasni.

(ii) Dunera-Chamba road *via* Katla.

(iii) Dunera-Chamba road *via* Katori.

(iv) Shahpur-Madhopur road *via* Khari.

(v) Bharoli-Bhandal road *via* Bhagi.

(c) *Checking Posts*-There were no checking posts during the State regime. Those established after merger do not appear to be at suitable places. Following checking posts are proposed to be set up on the routes fixed above:-

Bhaniar Gujars- Ghatasni on route No. 1, Katlu on route No. 2, Katori on route No. 3, Khairi on route No. 4 and Bhagi on route No. 5.

Chapter VII
Grazing Policy for Mandi and Nachan Forest Divisions

119. *Control of the movements of flocks and herds-*

 (a) *Registration and emmeration-* These have already been carried out, though in a loose manner and the record is maintained in a register *jamman Bandhi.* This record should be revised and brought up-to-date in lines with those suggested in Chapter V.

 (b) *Routes fixed or not* -The control exercised over the movements of foreign sheep and goats in Mandi State is examplary. Following routes have been fixed for the movements of Gaddis (including for foreign graziers inclusive of Mohammadan Gujars whether State resident or not):-

 (i) Ghata-Bhubu.

 (ii) Ghatta-Oot.

 (iii) Ghatta-Darbani.

 (iv) Bhaswah-Manghru.

 (v) Jhungi.

 (vi) Oot-Manghru

 (c) *Restrictions on the movements-* Suitable restrictions on the movements of flocks have also been prescribed in the Circular No. 1035/A.II.10 dated the .... January, 1934. These should be adhered to in future as well.

 (d) *Checking Posts-* Following checking posts had been fixed:-

 (1) Ghatta, (2) Bharwah, (3) Jhungi, (4) Oot. These posts will suit in future also.

Chapter VIII

Grazing Policy for Suket Forest Division

132. *Control on the movements of Flocks and Herds-*

 (a) *Registration and Enumeration-* Should be carried
out for the migratory and nomadic flocks and herds
on the lines suggested before.

 (b) *Routes fixed or not-*A mention of the main routes
used by the nomadic and migratory graziers has
been made in the Forest Settlement. But it has not
been made clear whether it is obligatory for the
flocks and herds to stick to these or not. However,
following routes are suggested to be fixed for future:-

 (i) Sai to Dehr and *vice versa.*

 (ii) Phirnu to Dehr and *vice versa.*

 (iii) Tatta-pani to Dehr and *vice versa.*

 (iv) Chuara-Phirnu-Tattapani route and *vice versa.*

 (v) Phirnu to Dehr along river and *vice versa.*

 (c) *Restrictions imposed on the movements-* No
restrictions whatsoever were imposed on the
movements of flocks during the State regime.
Restrictions attempted after merger have not been
strictly enforced. Restrictions suggested now should
be fully enforced. Following time limit is fixed for
traversing the above fixed routes:-

Route no. *i*   ..   ..   4 days.

Route no. *ii*   ..   ..   15 days.

Route no. *iii* ..   ..   6 days.

Route no. *iv*   ..   ..   7 days.

Route no. *v*   ..   ..   15 days.

 (d) *Checking Posts:-* There were no checking posts
during State regime. None have been established
after merger. The checking posts proposed to be
set up on the routes fixed above are Sai, Dehr,
Phirnu, Tatta-pani and Chaura.

Chapter IX

Grazing Policy for Jubbal Forest Division

149. *Control on the movements of flocks and herds-*

(a) *Registration and enumerations-* Has been carried out in the case of Gujars only. This needs revision as conditions have materially changed since the time when it was carried out. Owners of all the animals, migratory and nomadic, should be registered and their animals enumerated on the lines suggested in Chapter V.

(b) *Routes fixed or not:—*All the flocks and herds from Uttar Pradesh and Sirmur enter the State at Minus situated on the confluence of Sainj and Tons rivers. Some of them move along Sainj river on the main road to the forests of Kanda Range. They leave the main road at different points to enter different sub-valleys.

2. Others follow the road along Tons river upto Kirala where Shalvi-Garh stream meets the Tons river. Here they are divided into two parties.

3. One party moves along Shalvi-Garh stream to enter its various sub-valleys.

4. The other party follows the route along Tons upto Tiuni bridge in Uttar Pradesh. From Tiuni they move on the road along Pabar river and enter Jubbal territory near Moongia. They carry on along Pabar, local flocks entering different sub-valleys in the way, and the Kanwaras' flocks bound for Bashahr Division continue and leave Jubbal territory near Saura.

These routes are fixed since the State regime and should continue as such in future as well.

150. (a) *Restrictions imposed on the movements-* All the restrictions as suggested in Chapter V are already enforced since the State time and should continue for future. Only flocks that enter simply to pass through this division are those of Kanawars. Careful

watch is necessary to be kept on the movements of these flocks. If these flocks linger on for period more than that actually required for transit, they should be severely dealt with.

(b) *Checking Posts-* At present checking posts are situated at Minus for Jubbal, Bhundar for Keonthal, Pondran for Throach States. Now when Keonthal and Throach have been included in part in Jubbal, checking posts for these are no longer required. To suit the present requirements the following checking posts are suggested:-

(i) Minus on route No. 1.

(ii) Kiarla for route No. 2 and 3.

(iii) Moongia and Saura for route No. 4.

Chapter X

Grazing Policy of Nahan and Rajgarh Forest Divisions

171. *Control on the movements of flocks and herds:-*

(a) *Registration and enumeration-* The only nomadic graziers at present are Jammuwal and Pahari Gujars. For those who belong to Ambala district, it has been recommended to discontinue grazing of their animals. For the former, it has been recommended to allow grazing on permit system. It is, therefore, necessary to register them. This should be done on the lines suggested in Chapter V according to their leases, purchased during 1951-52.

(b) *Routes fixed or not-* No routes are fixed at present because the leases of '*paraos*' are auctioned and also because the entry of migratory flocks has been banned. Now when it has been recommended to remove the ban on the entry of migratory flocks and to replace the auction system of '*paraos*' by permit system, it is necessary to fix the routes. Following routes are, therefore, suggested-

(a) For buffaloes—

> *(i)* Rampur Ghat to Neri *via* Karganu and *vice versa;*
>
> *(ii)* Rajgarh to Nahan *via* Dadahu.

(b) Restrictions imposed on Movements- No restrictions, whatsoever, are imposed at present. In the light of proposals now made it is necessary to impose all the restrictions which have been suggested in Chapter V.

(c) Checking Posts- No checking posts exist at present. Following checking posts are suggested for future:-

> *(i)* Neri and Rampur Ghat on route No. *(i);*
>
> *(ii)* Dadahu on route No. *(ii).*

Chapter XII

Grazing Policy of Simla Forest Division

193. *Control on the Movements of Flocks*— *(i) Registration and enumeration*- Registration of each nomadic and migratory grazier has been done with respect to the grazing-run and number of animals to be grazed in that run. It is not in the form as suggested in this report. Registration and enumeration of the migratory and nomadic graziers should be carried out on the lines suggested in this report.

(ii) Routes fixed or not— Routes for the movements of the migratory and nomadic flocks were fixed neither during the State regime of integrating States nor are they fixed at present. Following routes are suggested to be fixed for future:-

> (1) Luri-Bhajji route *via* Pandhoa.
>
> (2) Route along Giri River *via* Khoru.
>
> (3) Country route *via* Punder (for Gujars).

All flocks entering in the Division for grazing or simply passing through must stick to these routes.

(iii) Restriction imposed on the movements or not- None were imposed during the regime of merged States and none

exist at present. In the light of proposals now made, it is necessary to impose all the restriction which had been suggested in Chapter V.

(iv) Checking Posts- No checking posts existed during the State regime nor do they exist now. Following posts are suggested for the future:-

    (a) Pandoha on route No. 1.
    (b) Khoru on route No. 2.
    (c) Randar for route No. 3.

Chapter XIII

Grazing Policy for Lower Bashahr Forest Division.

207. *Control on the movements of flocks and herds—*

    (a) Registration and enumeration- It has been done in the case of Gujjars only and not in the case of other migratory graziers and nomadic graziers. It should be done for all the graziers on the lines suggested in Chapter V.

    (b) Routes fixed or not- Routes are not fixed. Herds and flocks of animals follow any route they like during their movements to their summer and winter pastures. Following routes are suggested to be fixed.

For Gujjars- The Gujjars coming to Upper Paber from Dehra Dun side move on the route along Tons and Paber rivers. Those of Kumarsain who do not stay throughout the year enter the Division from Kulu and Suket side *via* Luri. Those who graze Nogli Range during winter follow the main Hindustan-Tibet Road. Following routes are, therefore, suggested to be fixed for them:-

    (i) Routes along Tons and Paber rivers via Rohru.
    (ii) Luri-Naula Road.
    (iii) Hindustan-Tibet Road (lower link).
    (iv) Hindustan-Tibet Road (upper link).

(c) Restrictions imposed on the movements— No restrictions whatsoever, on the movements of herd and flocks were imposed, during the State regime and none exist at present. Under the prevailing circumstances, it is imperative to impose restrictions on the movement of these animals. All restrictions suggested in Chapter V must be imposed.

(d) Checking posts- Neither checking posts existed before merger, nor do they exit now. Following checking posts are suggested for future:-

    (i) Rohru on route No. 1.

    (ii) Luri on route No. 2.

    (iii) Nogli on route No. 3.

    (iv) Taklech on route No. 4.

Chapter XIV

Grazing Policy of Upper Bashahr Forest Division

225. *Control on the movements of flocks and herds-*

    (a) Registration and emuneration- It has been done in the case of Gujars only and not in the case of other migratory graziers and nomadic graziers. It should be done for all the graziers on the lines suggested before in Chapter V.

Routes fixed or not- Routes are not fixed. Herds and flocks follow any route they like during their movements to summer and winter pastures. Following routes are suggested-

For Gujars-

    (i) Lower link of Hindustan Tibet Road *via* Rampur.

    (ii) Upper link of Hindustan-Tibet Road *via* Dharan-ghati.

(b) Restrictions imposed on the movements- No restrictions whatsoever on the movements of herds and flocks were imposed, either during the State regime, or are imposed at present. Under prevalent circumstances, it is

imperative to impose restrictions on the movements of these animals. All the restrictions suggested in Chapter V must be imposed.

(c) Checking posts- Neither checking posts existed before merger, nor do they exist now. Following checking posts are suggested for future:-

For Gujars:-

    (i) Rampur on route No. 1

    (ii) Dharan-ghati on route No. 2.

Appendix II

Gojari
Words, Sentences and Numerals

Numerals

Cardinal			Ordinal		
Ek	...	one	Pahila	...	first
Do	...	two	Duwoa	...	second
Trai	...	three	Triyya	...	third
Char	...	four	Chautha	...	fourth
Panj	...	five	Panjwa	...	fifth
Chha	...	six	Chhatha	...	sixth
Satt	...	seven	Satwa	...	seventh
Atth	...	eight	Attuwa	...	eighth
Nau	...	nine	Naunwa	...	nineth
Das	...	ten	Daswya	...	tenth
Bih	...	twenty	Adha	...	one half
Trih	...	thirty	Deudh	...	one & one half
Chali	...	forty	Paihli wari	...	1st time
Panja	...	fifty	Duwwi wari	...	2nd time

Satth	...	sixty	
Sathattor	...	seventy	
Asi	...	eighty	
Nabbe	...	ninety	
Sau	...	hundred	
Heizar	...	thousand	

Words*

I	...	Hu	Hand	... Hath
We	...	Ham	Nose	... Nakk
Thou	...	Tu	Mouth	... Muh
Thine	...	Tero	Ear	... Kann
Of you	...	Tharo	Head	... Sir
He	...	Wu	Back	... Mora
His	...	Uske	Gold	... Sona
Of them	...	Ungo	Father	... Aba (one's
Of me	...	Mero		own father)
Of us	...	Maharo		Bap (an-
Of thee	...	Tero		other's
You	...	Tam		father)
Your	...	Tharo	Of him	... Uske
They	...	Vi	Foot	... Pair
Eye	...	Akkh	Tooth	... Dand
Hair	...	Bal	Tongue	... Jib
Iron	...	Laho	Silver	... Chandi
Mother	...	Ama	Brother	... Bhai
Sister	...	Bahan, Bahain	Man	... Admi
Woman	...	Zanani	Wife	... Ran
Child	...	Bacha	Son	... Put (one's own son)
				Gadre (an-other's son)

Daughter	...	Ti	Slave	...	Gulam
God	...	Khuda	Devil	...	Shitan
Sun	...	Dih	Moon	...	Chann
Star	...	Tara	Fire	...	Agg
Water	...	Pani	House	...	Ghar
Horse	...	Koro	Cow	...	Ga
Dog	...	Kuto	Cat	...	Billi
Cock	...	Kukur	Ass	...	Khoto
Go	...	Ja	Eat	...	Kha
Sit	...	Bais	Come	...	Au
Beat	...	Mar	Stand	...	Khaloho
Die	...	Mar	Give	...	De
Run	...	Dor	Up	...	Upar
Near	...	Nere	Down	...	Bunh
Far	...	Dur	Before	...	Age
Behind	...	Pichhe	Who	...	Kon
What	...	Ke	Why	...	Kiyo
And	...	Hor	But	...	Magar
If	...	Agar	Yes	...	Ha
No	...	Nai	Alas	...	Hae

A father	...	Bap
Of a father	...	Bap-ko
To a father	...	Bap-na
From a father	...	Bap thu
A daughter	...	Ti
Of a daughter	...	Ti-ko
To a daughter	...	Ti-na
From a daughter	..	Ti-thu
A good man	...	Ek chango admi
Of a good man	...	Ekan chango admi-go
A bad boy	...	Ek pairo gadro

A bad girl	...	Ek pairi gadri
Good	...	Chango
Better	...	Much chango
Best	...	Sara-thu-chango
High	...	Uchcho
Higher	...	Much Uchcho
Highest	...	Sara-thu-uchcho
I am	...	Hu-ho
Thou art	...	Tu hai
He is	...	Wu hai
We are	...	Ham ha
You are	...	Tam he
They are	...	Vi he
I was	...	He tho thou
He was	...	Wu the
We were	...	Ham tha
You were	...	Tam tha
Go	...	Ja
Going	...	Jato
Gone	...	Gio-ri

Sentences

What is your name?	...	Tero na ke hai?
How old is this horse?	...	Yu koro kitno-ek baro hai?
How far is it from here to Kashmir.	...	Itu Kashmir kitni-ek-dur hai
I have walked a long way today.	...	Mai aaj much pendo kario-hai.
I have beaten his son with many stripes.	...	Mai mareo us-ko gadro apni kamchi nal.
He is grazing cattle on the top of the hill	...	Wu us taka-gitt choti-par apna chokkara-na chara lagovi.

His brother is taller than his sister.	...	Us-ko bhai us-ki behan-thu lammo hai.
My father lives in that small house.	...	Mero bap us nikka ghar-ma raha.
Give this rupee to him.	...	Yu rupaya us-wa de.
Take this rupee from him	...	Vi rupaya us-thu le-la.
Draw water from the well	...	Khu-thu pani charo.
Walk before me.	...	Mere agge agge chal.
From whom did you buy that?	...	Te wup kis-thu mul lie-vi hai
From a shopkeeper of the village	...	Gra-ka hatiala-thu.

---

*Grieson, G.A., *Linguistic Survey of India,* Vol. IX, Part IV; 1909, Reprint, Delhi, 1967.

Select Bibliography

Bhardwaj A.N., *Tisri Gujar Tribal Conference,* Pathankot (Hindi); Salogra (Solan); 1960.

Bingley A.H., *History, Caste and Culture of Jats and Gujars,* 1899; Reprint Delhi (2nd Edn.), 1978.

Borman Hans Herbert, *Shepherding in Dhaula Dhar;* Palampur, 1980.

Crooke William, *Islam in India—The Customs of the Musalmans of India,* 1921; Reprint, New Delhi, 1972.

————, *Natives of North India;* London, 1907.

Cunningham Alexandar, *The Ancient Geography of India,* 1924; Reprint, Varanasi, 1963.

Denzil Charles Ibbetson, J., *Punjab Census Report;* Lahore, 1881.

Frederick Bath, *Nomads of South Persia;* London, 1961.

Grierson G.A., *Linguistic Survey of India,* Vol. IX, Part IV; Reprint, Delhi, 1967.

Goetz Herman, *The Early Wooden Temples of Chamba;* Leiden, 1955.

Handa, O.C., *Textiles, Costumes and Ornaments of the Western Himalaya;* New Delhi, 1998.

Hussain Majid, *Geography of Jammu and Kashmir;* New Delhi, 1985.

Jistu D.C., *A Study of Gujars—A Nomadic Tribe in Mahasu District, Himachal Pradesh;* New Delhi, 1962 (Unpublished).

Lal B.B., *Palaeoliths from the Beas and Bangana Valley— Punjab—Ancient India,* Vol. XII.

Lawrence Walter, *Valley of Kashmir;* Srinagar (J&K), 1967.

Leydon John, *Babar*

Munshi K.M., *Glory that Was Gurjardesa (A.D. 550-1300);* Bombay, 1955.

Nag D.S., *Tribal Economy;* Delhi, 1958.

Negi T.S., *Scheduled Tribes of Himachal Pradesh—A Profile;* Meerut, 1976.

Nesfield John C., *Brief View of the Caste System of the North Western Provinces and Oudh;* Reprint, Delhi, 1969.

Ohri V.C. (Ed.). *Pre-history of Himachal Pradesh;* 1979.

Ray Chaudhary S.P., *Land and Soil;* Delhi, 1966.

Risley, *Encyclopaedia of Religion and Ethics;* New York, 1953.

Rose, H.A. (Comp), *A Glossary of Tribes and Castes of the Punjab and NWFP;* Lahore, 1914-19.

Seligman Edwin R.A. (Ed.) *Encyclopaedia of Social Sciences;* New York, 1953.

Shashi S.S., *The Nomads of Himalaya;* New Delhi, 1979.

————, *Encyclopaedia of Indian Tribes—Himachal Pradesh and Northern Highlands* (Vol. VI); New Delhi, 1994.

Singh K.S., (Ed.), *People of India, Vol. III—Scheduled Castes and Tribes;* New Delhi, 1994.

————, *People of India, Vol. XXIV—Himachal Pradesh;* New Delhi, 1996.

Singh R.L., (Ed.), *India—A Regional Geography;* Varanasi, 1971.

Smith V.A., *Early History of India;* London, 1908.

Verma, V., *The Emergence of Himachal Pradesh;* New Delhi, 1955.

————, *Gaddis of Dhauladhar: A Transhumant Tribe of the Himalayas;* New Delhi, 1966.

————, *Pangi: A Tribal Habitat of Mid-Himalaya;* New Delhi, 1997.

Verrier Elwyn, *A New Deal for Tribal India;* New Delhi, 1963.

Government Publications

(i) Himachal Pradesh Administration/Government

Economics and Statistics Directorate. *A Socio-economic Survey of Gujars;* Shimla, 1983.

Forest Department (Parmar B.S.). *Report on the Grazing Problems and Policy of Himachal Pradesh;* Shimla, 1959.

————, *Annual Administration Report for the Year 1994-95;* Shimla, 1996. (Also reports for the previous years).

————, *Himachal Pradesh Forest Statistics,* 1996; Shimla, 1997. (Also of previous years).

General Administration. *Annual Administration Report for the year 1964-65;* Shimla, 1965. (Also for the years 1957 to 1963).

Institute of Public Administration. *A Study on Different Aspects of Minorities in Himachal Pradesh with Special Reference to Gujars;* Shimla, 1994.

Tribal Development Department. *Annual Tribal Sub-Plan, 1996-97;* Shimla, 1996.

————, *Annual Tribal Sub-Plan, 1996-97—ITDP-wise Schematic Budgeted Outlays;* Shimla, 1996.

University of Agriculture, Palampur (Chauhan, S.K.). *Credit Requirement in Dairy Enterprise—A Financial Study of Gujjars in Kangra district of Himachal Pradesh;* Palampur, 1982 (Unpublished).

Himachal Pradesh Institute of Tribal Development. *Tribal Development — Appraisal and Alternatives;* New Delhi, 1998.

(ii) Government of India, Ministry of Home Affairs

Pal, R.C. (Ed.), *Census Reports for the years 1911 to 1991. A Village Survey— Maingal (Chamba),* Himachal Pradesh, Vol. XX, Part VI, No. 27; New Delhi, 1964.

Parliament of India Secretariat, Lok Sabha. *Constituent Assembly Debates,* Vol. III; New Delhi, 1989.

(iii) Government of Punjab

Gazetteer of Kangra District, Pt. I., *Kangra,* Reprint, New Delhi, 1994.

Punjab District Gazetteer, Vol. VIIIA, Shimla District Part A, Lahore, 1904.

Barnes G.C. (Ed.). *Report on the Kangra Settlement, 1850-52;* Lahore, 1855.

(iv) Government of United Provinces

Walton H.G. (Ed.). *District Gazetteer of United Provinces of Agra & Oudh;* Allahabad, 1911.

Index

1. Proud descendants of Gurjaras, once a mighty and powerful Ruling race.

2. On way to the market with day's milk yield.

3.   A typical Gujar residence-cum-cattleshed called *kotha*.

4.   In repose.

5.   A snapshot of Gujar habitat.

6.   Portrait of a Gujar family.

7. Gujar *belle* full of charm and innocence.

8.   Her daily routine—to sell milk.

9. *Taxus baccata* appropriately called *Brahmi* or *Rakhal* fights cancer.

10. Meal time.

11. Wind of change—their clothes proclaim—is blowing.